THE
CATHOLIC
RESPONSE

THE CATHOLIC RESPONSE

REVISED AND UPDATED

Very Reverend Peter M. J. Stravinskas, Ph.D., S.T.D.

Our Sunday Visitor Publishing Division
Our Sunday Visitor, Inc.
Huntington, Indiana 46750

Portions of this book appeared in different form in *Our Sunday Visitor* (co-authored with William J. Sweeney) and in the *National Catholic Register,* whose permission to use this material is gratefully acknowledged. The majority of the Scripture texts used in this work are taken from the *New American Bible,* copyright © 1970 by the Confraternity of Christian Doctrine, Washington, D.C., all rights reserved, and the Catholic edition of the *Revised Standard Bible,* copyright © 1966 by the Division of Christian Education of the National Council of Churches of Christ in the United States of America, all rights reserved. Quotations from documents of the Second Vatican Council are taken from *Vatican II: The Conciliar and Post Conciliar Documents,* copyright © 1975 by Costello Publishing Co., Inc., and Reverend Austin Flannery, O.P.; all rights reserved. Every reasonable effort has been made to determine copyright holders. If any copyrighted materials have been inadvertently used in this work without proper credit being given in one form or another, please notify Our Sunday Visitor in writing so that future printings of this work may be corrected accordingly.

Our Sunday Visitor Publishing Division
Our Sunday Visitor, Inc.
200 Noll Plaza
Huntington, IN 46750

ISBN: 0-87973-913-4
LCCCN: 00-140003

Cover design by Rebecca Heaston
PRINTED IN THE UNITED STATES OF AMERICA

*In gratitude for nearly two decades of priestly
support and friendship, and most especially for
his inspiration and assistance throughout its
writing, this book is respectfully dedicated to
the Rev. Msgr. Joseph C. Shenrock, S.T.L., Ph.D.,
pastor of Blessed Sacrament Church in Trenton,
New Jersey, and director of the Trenton
Diocesan Commission on Ecumenical and
Interreligious Affairs:
"That all may be one" (John 17:21).*

Contents

Acknowledgments • 9

Preface • 11

Introduction to the Revised Edition • 13

Introduction to the First Edition • 17

1 • How Does God Reveal Himself? • 21

2 • What Must I Do to Be Saved? • 33

3 • Is the Catholic Church Christian? • 45

4 • Who Rules the Church? • 55

5 • Did Christ Establish the Priesthood? • 65

6 • Do Catholics Worship Mary and the Other Saints? • 75

7 • Is the Mass Biblical? • 87

8 • Can Priests Forgive Sins? • 99

9 • Where Do We Go From Here? • 109

Epilogue • 117

Appendix: A New Apologetic for Today's Needs • 125

Bibliography • 127

Notes • 137

Acknowledgments

The review of the manuscript was the work of many friends, whose interest and contributions were so very helpful. Among them I must list: The Reverend Brian Mead, the Reverend Perry Dodds, the Reverend Dennis Day, the Reverend Richard Carrington, the Reverend Robert Batule, the Reverend Thomas Mathes, Michael Morrow, Wilfredo Comellas, John Barres, Rabbi Yehuda Levin, and the Reverend Stephen Bosso, S.S.L.

A special word of thanks is due the Reverend Damien Dougherty, O.F.M., S.S.L., for his painstaking efforts to see that the Scriptures were used correctly, honorably, and with integrity.

A final note of appreciation is made of the work of my longtime secretary, Mrs. Patricia Adamo, whose pleasant attitude prevailed, even when multiple rewrites made her job that much more difficult.

The revised edition has been significantly improved by the insights and suggestions of the Reverend Nicholas L. Gregoris and the welcome references to the *Catechism of the Catholic Church* added by the Reverend Michael Redmann, both clerics of the Diocesan Oratory of St. Philip Neri in Mount Pocono, Pennsylvania, which community I have the honor of serving as provost.

Acknowledgments

Preface

Our Holy Father John Paul II has called for a new evangelization for the millennium that we have now entered. Evangelization is sharing the good news of Jesus Christ with those who don't know Him or who need to know Him better. There are millions of people in our own country who are confused about their relationship with God and the Church He founded, through His Son, Jesus. The Holy Father wants us to reach out in loving ways to inactive Catholics and to those who have been attracted to Fundamentalism. He also wants to strengthen the faith of Catholics so that they are not easy prey to Fundamentalist groups that constantly seem to be proselytizing members of the Catholic Faith.

John Paul II spoke beautifully during his homily in St. Louis on January 27, 1999, when he addressed those who were separated from the practice of their faith. "Christ is seeking you out and inviting you back to the community of faith. Is this not the moment for you to experience the joy of returning to the Father's House? In some cases there might still be obstacles to Eucharistic participation; in some cases there may be memories to be healed; in all cases there is the assurance of God's love and mercy."

As Father Stravinskas says, there are a variety of reasons why Catholics might be tempted to embrace Fundamentalism or some Bible-based church. They may have been scandalized by sinful members of our Church, especially among the clergy or Religious. They may be attracted by a deceptively simple message that some Fundamentalist preachers give. Not being connected appropriately to their own Catholic Faith they may feel more in touch with Jesus personally, as presented by the Bible-based church. When Catholics are proselytized at work or in the neighborhood, they need a solid understanding of how to answer the many questions that their Fundamentalist friends and neighbors may ask them. This book by Father Stravinskas gives a clear explanation of the Catholic position regarding many aspects of Christian faith. The brief Epilogue (the letter to Bob and Laurie, good Catholics who are being affected by Fundamentalism) will be most helpful to many.

We believe that the Catholic Faith has the fullness of the teaching of Jesus, not just a part of it. There is an answer to every question that can be raised against our Faith. This book makes a significant contribution in helping people to engage in dialogue about unanswered questions they might have. In addition to reason, however, we pray for ever-stronger faith and the grace from Jesus that makes our faith possible.

In our search for God we must be seeking truth, using right reason and the intellect God gave us. But we know that ultimately our faith depends on God's gift of the grace to believe. We ask God to increase our faith and to give others the grace to believe as well.

Most Rev. Michael J. Sheehan
Archbishop of Santa Fe

Introduction to the Revised Edition

The French have a proverb that translates thus: "He who bites the Pope's nose, dies." That aphorism embodies in a kind of "down home" way some profound wisdom, grounded in sound theology and history. Simply put, Christ's promise to establish His Church on the rock of St. Peter and to remain with His Church until the end of time will not fail — in spite of sinners from within and enemies from without. At any rate, that expression came to mind as we were preparing this revised edition of *The Catholic Response.* Let me explain.

The first edition came about because of some very particular circumstances, which might be helpful to rehearse. In the early 1980s, a televangelist named the Reverend Jimmy Swaggart made his debut, with diatribes against the Catholic Church as his stock in trade and weak Catholics as his target audience. In addition to his broadcasts, he began producing pamphlets and, most especially, his famous *Letter to My Catholic Friends,* wherein he attempted to discuss just about every objection he had to the Catholic Faith. A colleague and I responded with a sixteen-week series of articles in *Our Sunday Visitor.* Reader response was immediate and positive, encouraging us to publish the work as a book for handy reference.

Over the past fifteen years, it has been most gratifying to be told by literally hundreds of people that *The Catholic Response* either kept them within the Church or brought them back — or did the same for a relative or friend. And although Jimmy Swaggart, because of his personal vitriol, a fall from grace, and his subsequent fall from public favor, is no longer a key player in Fundamentalist proselytism, there is still no shortage of would-be successors for his mantle. Therefore, the advisability of a new edition.

This edition, however, is not just a reprint but also improved in many ways. First of all, the basic text is enriched by references to the *Catechism of the Catholic Church.* Readers are thus brought into direct contact with *the* official explanation of Catholic teaching. Secondly, many times over the past several years, Pope John Paul II has encouraged a revival of the apostolate of apologetics; included as an appendix here is one of his most explicit talks in this regard, providing novice and veteran apologists alike with a program of action and a "shot in the arm" for their efforts. It was also deemed worthwhile to include a list of resources from both the print and electronic media to assist readers in delving deeper into the questions touched upon in the body of the text; these come from the Magisterium itself and also from authors who are renowned for their orthodoxy and comprehensibility. Finally, I am honored by the Preface of a longtime friend, the Most Reverend Michael Sheehan of Santa Fe. Archbishop Sheehan is known not only for his interest in apologetics but also for his active work in that field, producing dozens of excellent brief — but comprehensive — treatises on a host of topics that generally find their way into discussions or debates with our Fundamentalist brothers and sisters.

More than a century and a half ago, the English historian and statesman Macaulay expressed well the sum and substance of our French proverb when he wrote that the Catholic Church "may still exist in undiminished vigour when some traveller from New Zealand shall, in the midst of a vast solitude, take his stand on a broken arch of London Bridge to sketch the ruins of St. Paul's." Such an insight should not make us Catholics haughty or arrogant for, as Abraham Heschel put it so well, "all that we own, we owe." In other words, the preservation of the Church in the truth and in glory is the work and the will of Christ and His Holy Spirit. It is but a grace and a privilege given to us at this moment in time to serve as a link in that chain which preserves what the Roman Canon aptly speaks of as "the Faith which comes to us from the Apostles." The misguided and the malevolent come and go throughout the ages; only Christ's Church prevails as His immaculate Bride and our loving Mother until He comes again.

At the dawning of a new millennium, I wish to dedicate this book and all our efforts at "the new evangelization" to Our Lady of the New Advent. May she who brought about the Lord's First Advent in the flesh inspire us by her example of Gospel fidelity and by her powerful intercession to do our part to prepare for His Second Advent in glory when He will come to take His holy Church, which remains on earth, to join the Church in heaven, where the wedding feast of the Lamb has already begun.

Introduction to the First Edition

A convert-friend of mine always corrects me when I speak of "Fundamentalists," meaning those Christians who interpret Scripture literally. She likes the word "fundamentalist" and would like to apply it to the Catholic Church. In fact, she says she joined the Church precisely because the Church is "fundamentalistic," in the sense that all the basic, or fundamental, doctrines are preserved and taught by the Catholic Church. This is a very good point that needs to be made from time to time; however, words have a way of taking on a life of their own, and no matter what my friend says or thinks, it seems to me that "Fundamentalism" means — and will mean for a long time to come — biblical literalism.

Why a *Catholic Response* to the Fundamentalists? They are a large and growing segment of American religious life. They are vocal and aggressive, frequently virulently anti-Catholic. They are generally misinformed on a variety of fronts: the nature of Divine Revelation; Catholic life and doctrine; even secular history. More often than not, they are as lacking in charity as they are in understanding — if for no other reason than the fact that so many of them are fallen-away Catholics.

Of course, a critical question to raise is: "Why are their numbers swelling, particularly from Catholic ranks?" Their approach appears simple, absolute, and uncomplicated; but appearances can be deceiving. St. Augustine said the whole of Christian life could be summed up in the maxim "Love, and then do whatever you will." However, the mature believer gradually realizes that simple theories are the hardest to put into practice.

Another reason for the crossover of Catholics to Fundamentalism is due to the theological confusion of post-conciliar Catholicism in the United States. It is no accident that Fundamentalism held no attraction for Catholics when we had our own house in order; conversely, when theologians and clergy began to question traditional teachings and then to teach speculative theories as valid alternatives to authentic Catholic doctrine, young Catholics had their faith shaken. Searching for a rock of faith, they stumbled onto the Fundamentalists. Young Catholics, without good formation or information, were easily swayed. Now many are beginning to see that the apparent simplicity may not have been better after all. Furthermore, many are also taking a second look at their original faith heritage as the storm clouds settle and the Pope once more assures the faithful that they have a right to have the true Faith presented to them by their clergy, without distortion and in total fidelity to the Tradition of the Church.

This book, then, should serve a variety of audiences. Its approach is ecumenical, not apologetical in a negative sense. Ecumenism involves being open to the other; presenting one's faith honestly and forthrightly; entering into a dialogue aimed at mutual understanding and done with respect for the dignity of the other. An apologetical approach since the Protestant Reformation was often more defensive and directed toward the goal of conversion. This book does not seek to convert Fundamentalists to Catholicism (although I would be delighted if it helped some come to the fullness of Christian faith found only in the Catholic Church); the primary thrust of this work is to provide Catholics with the answers they need to maintain and articulate their own faith if they are engaged in dialogue with Fundamentalists or if they are being pursued by them. This book also seeks to take seriously the questions of fallen-away Catholics, even if somewhat belatedly, in the hope that they will respond to God's grace and come back home.

The methodology of the book can be seen as a paradigm for ecumenical dialogue in general. First of all, Christian dialogue must be carried on with charity. It is important to presume goodwill on the part of all, as well as a basic love for the Lord Jesus Christ. Charity will also require that we Catholics not place any burdens on our dialogue partners beyond that which the truth of the Catholic Faith demands.

Christian dialogue is advanced with knowledge. In the sharing of knowledge, it is essential that the Scriptures be honored; one should never fall into the trap of depreciating the Sacred Scriptures simply because one's dialogue partner overstates the case. It is then necessary to lead the other to an appreciation of Sacred Tradition, which, together with Scripture, forms a unified font of Divine Revelation. Knowledge also involves common sense and grows through extensive and ongoing reading of Scripture, the Fathers of the Church,[1] the pronouncements of the Magisterium,[2] and contemporary theological discussion. Finally, knowledge is best imparted when one explains his or her faith, rather than defending it or attacking the faith of the other person. Christian dialogue is pushed forward with conviction. Our explanations of Catholic teaching must never be cold, aloof, or impersonal; they must take their inspiration from the Lord Himself as He interpreted the Scriptures for the disciples on the road to Emmaus (cf. Lk 24:13-35). The result was that they found their "hearts burning" within them. We must never hesitate to share with others how much our life in Christ and in His Church means to us and how much it can mean to them.

Charity, knowledge, and conviction are the necessary ingredients for a worthwhile ecumenical encounter. I hope I have been faithful to these criteria in these pages. If so, the Holy Spirit will be able to use this book to bring people to faith for the first time, to revive faith for the lapsed, or to deepen the faith of the committed.

Fides quaerens intellectum ("Faith seeking understanding") is a cardinal principle of Catholic theology. We never have all the answers; with St. Paul, "we walk by faith, not by sight" (2 Cor 5:7). But it is always right to ask questions, in order to understand better. Or, as Cardinal Newman put it, "Ten thousand difficulties do not make one doubt."[3] This book raises questions just so that the single doubt will never surface.

The ultimate goal of this book[4] is that a spirit of honest inquiry will bring the reader to take as his own that beautiful prayer of the possessed boy's father: "I believe, Lord; help my unbelief" (Mk 9:24).

1

How Does God Reveal Himself?

What is revelation? Revelation is the medium and the message by which Almighty God discloses to us the mystery of His own divine life and of our life in Him. For nearly sixteen centuries of Christian history, such a definition would have posed little or no problem. Individuals would have argued about the *interpretation* of the revealed message, but not about its content or sources. (Cf. *Catechism of the Catholic Church*, nn. 50-51.)

Then came Martin Luther, an Augustinian friar, biblical scholar, and ecclesiastical reformer. Luther was an exemplary religious and a zealous reformer, but when his efforts at needed reform were met with ecclesiastical indifference or hostility, his faith in the Church was shaken, leading him to condemn Church authority and the whole concept of Sacred Tradition. This eventually found expression in the formula of *sola Scriptura* ("Scripture alone") as a norm for Christian life and doctrine. (Cf. CCC nn. 80-82.)

This approach to revelation was an absolute novelty; never before in Judaism or Christianity had the position been seriously advanced that the Scriptures were self-explanatory documents, not requiring a body of Tradition or a living faith community to interpret. In the theological skirmishes that ensued, positions were caricatured and solidified to the point where the impression was created at the popular level that Catholics opted for Tradition while Protestants accepted only Scripture. Actually, the polemics involved an even more negative conclusion: that Catholics were against Scripture, and that Protestants were against Tradition. Such a development was most unfortunate.

In the more peaceful era that formed the backdrop for the Second Vatican Council, the bishops sought to put an end to the perceived rivalry between Scripture and Tradition. In their Dogmatic Constitution on Divine Revelation (*Dei Verbum*), the Council Fathers indicated that the Church teaches that Sacred Tradition and Sacred Scripture form one sacred deposit of the Word of God. This is due to the fact that both stem from one source of revelation: God Himself, Who wishes to share with His People all that is necessary for their salvation.[1] This process reached a high-water mark in the life of His Son, as we learn in the Letter to the Hebrews: "In times past, God spoke in fragmentary and varied ways to our fathers through the prophets; in this, the final age, he has spoken to us through his Son" (1:1f). The Son's work of revelation finds continuation and fulfillment in His Church (cf. Eph 1:22f; Col 1:18, 24), so that there is no dichotomy between Christ and His Church. The revelation begun by the Father through the prophets is continued by the Incarnate Word and never ceases as the Church operates under the guidance of the Holy Spirit, growing in her understanding of the content of the Deposit of Faith. (Cf. CCC nn. 77-80, 84.)

If it is true that our God has wished to reveal Himself, then one must believe that He has set a process in motion whereby that revelation can take place with total confidence. Such enlightenment has traditionally been viewed as a work of the Holy Spirit. When Luther challenged the notion that the Church could be a faithful repository and transmitter of Divine Revelation, at root he was questioning the Holy Spirit more than the Church — although he would have vociferously denied such an allegation. The point remains, however, that God has chosen to use normally fallible instruments (human language and human beings) to hand on an infallible message (cf. 2 Cor 4:7). (Cf. CCC nn. 39-43.)

Many years ago an excellent book on the Sacred Scriptures was written by Jean Lévie, entitled *The Word of God in the Words of Men.* The thesis of the work was that there was a dynamic interaction between divine and human elements in the formation of the Bible, and in all revelation. To understand better this dynamic, it will be helpful to examine the precise nature of Scripture and Tradition, and their basic interrelatedness.

Some believers take the Bible for granted, in the sense that they see it as a volume delivered to the Christian community many years ago in finished form. The Scriptures, however, were written by many people over an extended period of time. The composition of the Old Testament writings alone took more than a millennium to complete. The history of salvation from the dawn of creation to the apostolic age was a history of progressive revelation; from the death of the last apostle until the final days at the Lord's Second Coming will be a history of progressive growth in human understanding of the divine mystery. That is why Jesus' promise of the Holy Spirit as our advocate and guide was so important (cf. Jn 14:26). Thus we would never be left orphans but would continue to be enlightened and led to a deeper comprehension of God's will and teachings. With this background in mind, we can better study the formation of Scripture in the early Church.

In his now-famous letter to his "Catholic friends,"[2] Jimmy Swaggart states that "the Bible was never delivered to the Catholic Church by God." In a certain respect, this statement is true — for the Bible, and the New Testament in particular, was not delivered by God to the Church, nor to Israel before her. No, the Hebrew Scriptures were written by the Jewish community over a thousand-year span by a wide range of sacred authors, putting "the Word of God" into "the words of men" — all under divine inspiration. The same pattern was continued in the Christian Dispensation, as the apostles and other members of the early Church were responsible for the writings found in the New Testament.

The New Testament writings were based on Jesus' disciples' remembrance of Him, the recollection of His teachings as they had been handed down, reports, and personal testimony. These writings were produced, of course, with the aid and inspiration of the same Holy Spirit, Who had guided the formation of the Old Testament. The Christian Scriptures, then, were not given intact by Christ to His disciples before His ascension to the Father, but took shape within and through the life and development of the early Church. In fact, most biblical scholars hold that even the earliest works of the New Testament, such as Paul's Letter to the Galatians, can be dated no earlier than A.D. 48 to 50, some fifteen to twenty years after Jesus' Death and Resurrection. Many speculate that the Gospel of Mark was not written before the year 65, and the Gospel of John perhaps as late as 110. Was there then a void between the Resurrection and the first written documents of Christian faith? Not at all, for the proclamation of the Gospel message was taking place in and through the Church, which was born with the coming of the Spirit and sent on mission for Christ at Pentecost (cf. Acts 2).

In order to appreciate the development of Scripture in

the early Church, it is essential to realize the importance of oral tradition in that day and age, and hence for the Christian community as well. When Jesus commissioned the apostles to "make disciples of all the nations" (Mt 28:19), they had only one tool ready at hand: preaching. It was oral communication that enabled the good news of Jesus to spread to the ends of the known world. Because of the expense and scarcity of written material in the first century, the early Christians (like the rest of the world) relied upon memory (which was a highly developed human faculty at that time and still is in the Near East) and word of mouth to pass on information of importance from one person to another and from one generation to another. Therefore, it should come as no surprise that Christ's message was not immediately preserved in written form, since oral transmission was, by far, the more usual, accessible, and effective means of communication. (Cf. CCC nn. 76, 126.)

A second and very logical reason existed for the disciples to use only word of mouth for the spreading of the Word of God: the belief that the Parousia (Christ's Second Coming) would occur within the lifetime of the apostles. In describing the coming of the Son of Man, Matthew's Gospel notes that "this generation will not pass away till all these things take place" (24:34). If the Parousia were imminent, why bother writing history that no one would ever get a chance to read? Even more to the point, the disciples saw no need to waste time on such an enterprise but thought it imperative to preach God's message as widely and quickly as possible — since time was so short, as they thought. It was not until some years later, as the Church grew and developed and realized that the Second Coming would be delayed, that putting the Lord's teachings into written form took on some meaning and even some urgency.

Even after the oral tradition was committed to written form, Scripture was never considered to be the sole source of God's Word and revelation. John's Gospel tells us quite plainly that "Jesus performed many other signs as well — signs not recorded here — in the presence of his disciples" (20:30). The Lord's work and teaching were obviously more extensive than what was recorded in Scripture, for the evangelist also notes with some hyperbole: "There are still many other things that Jesus did, yet if they were written about in detail, I doubt there would be room enough in the entire world to hold the books to record them" (Jn 21:25). The early Church, then, had both an oral and a written record on which to draw and thus passed on the revelation of God in Christ as Scripture and Tradition.

This assertion is not mere wishful thinking, for it is evident that the early Church accepted various traditions and teachings that were not recorded in writing. In his Second Letter to the Thessalonians, St. Paul exhorts the community there to "hold fast to the traditions you received from us, either by our word or by letter" (2:15). While not enumerating them in his letter, Paul nonetheless advises the Church at Thessalonica to "hold fast to the traditions" it had received from Silvanus, Timothy, and himself.

Some Fundamentalists have problems with the concept of change. Exaggeration for effect has led at least one to charge that "Catholic traditions change from year to year." A basic confusion emerges here between Tradition (in the singular, with a capital "T") and traditions (plural and lower case). It is crucial to distinguish between Sacred Tradition, which consists of those teachings and forms of worship that have been handed down and developed from Jesus and the apostles, and ecclesiastical traditions, which are man-made regulations (like Friday abstinence), established by the Church to help

26

Christians more fully understand and become involved in God's truths and teachings. While traditions may change with the needs of God's People, Sacred Tradition (like Sacred Scripture) is unchangeable. The traditions are designed to keep the Church faithful to the Tradition. Change is not a negative factor or stigma to be feared in Christian life. The decision to preach the Gospel to Gentiles and not require adherence to the Mosaic Law was a significant change at the very outset of the Christian experience (cf. Acts 15). The establishment of deacons, Sunday worship, forms of community governance, attitudes toward the State, and so many other matters can be used as illustrations (right within the Scriptures themselves) of how the early Church felt comfortable and qualified to make changes, where necessary, in the day-to-day living of the Christian Faith.[3] This was so because they saw how intimately tied to each other are the Spirit and the Church, as we read in Acts: "It is the decision of the Holy Spirit, and ours too . . ." (15:28). In other words, there is a connection — even an identification — between the Spirit and the Church. This identity guarantees that the changes made preserve the Church in truth and fidelity. (Cf. CCC nn. 78, 81, 83, 95, 113.)

Just as the Church and Tradition are interconnected, so too is there a necessary relationship between the Church, Scripture, and Tradition. When viewed from a clear historical perspective, Sacred Tradition cannot be disregarded without also denying the validity of Scripture itself, since both spring from one unified source of revelation, namely, God in Christ. In John's Gospel we learn that the Holy Spirit will remind the disciples of all that Jesus had told them (cf. Jn 14:26). As already noted, that same Gospel tells us that Jesus did many other things that were not recorded. If God is true to His promise — and He is — then the disciples could not have forgotten or ignored unwritten Christian Tradition, nor could they have lost Jesus' teachings. This is due, not to their own effectiveness or reliability, but to God, Who wishes to reveal Himself and so guides and guarantees the process of revelation throughout. The Christian Faith, then, was handed on to trustworthy men to teach, in accordance with the instructions given to Timothy (cf. 2 Tim 2:2).

Acceptance of this notion is essential to acceptance of Christianity itself, for if the revelatory process is not infallible, no doctrine (not even the Person of Jesus Himself) can make a claim on the mind or heart of any human being, as the rational basis of faith is destroyed. While it is true that an act of faith requires a leap into the dark, it is always a reasoned leap and never unreasoned or irrational. An act of faith, to be a human act, must take in both human faculties: reason and will. To suggest otherwise is to ask for a less-than-human response to the divine call to faith.

Reason and intellect are divine gifts, just as is an attitude of trust, and they should never be despised, lest one find himself rejecting that which the Lord God found to be "very good" (Gen 1:31).

The goal of revelation, and Christian preaching as well, is that "all men [will be] saved and come to know the truth" (1 Tim 2:4). That truth comes through the Church, which was made the authorized custodian of Christ's teachings as Jesus promised His disciples that the Holy Spirit would guide them into all truth (cf. Jn 16:13). Jimmy Swaggart, however, contends that "the Catholic Church cannot guarantee the inspiration of the Bible nor speak for God in any other manner." It seems that Swaggart has confused "inspiration" (divine guidance) with "inerrancy" (accuracy or truthfulness), but actually the Church can guarantee both, for the same reason. Not only was the entire New Testament written within the Church — for to what living body did the evangelists and other writers belong, if not the Church? — but the Church also decided which writings were inspired and then incorporated them into the canon of the Bible. The Church was given the gift of the Spirit, wrote under the influence of the same Spirit, and then assembled the works to be normative for Christian faith. The inescapable reality throughout is the Church. As St. Augustine said, "But I would not believe in the Gospel, had not the authority of the Catholic Church already moved me."[4] (Cf. CCC n. 120.)

The question of canonicity requires special attention. Canonicity is that quality ascribed by the Church to certain writings, whereby she declares them to be inspired and part of the Bible. Therefore, all canonical books are inspired by God. Not all inspired works are necessarily canonical, but we know that any such books that might exist contain no information needed for salvation, since God's revelation in Christ was absolute and complete.

How did the canon of the Bible come to be formed? It seems that there was a canon of the Hebrew Scriptures before the time of Christ, but we have no clear evidence for the date or place of such a decision. Not until the first century of the Christian era do we find a formal decision on the Jewish canon. As a result of external pressures from the Roman conquerors and internal pressures from the various sects within Judaism (including the Christians), Jewish religious authorities saw the necessity for a clearer self-definition at the Council of Jamnia. At Jamnia the definitive sources of Jewish revelation were settled on, so that future confrontations or disputations could be carried on within clearly defined parameters.

The Christian Scriptures were acknowledged by common consensus until the sixteenth century. Then Luther decided to delete some books from the Old Testament and the New Testament; in the seventeenth century, however, Protestants returned Luther's New Testament deletions to their canon of the Bible. The Council of Trent, in response to the Reformers, decreed the finished canon of the Bible, reaffirming the Tradition of the Church, which had developed centuries earlier. One should note that the Church at Trent did not make a new list of accepted texts, but merely solemnly defined the existing and long-standing Tradition. In times of peace, neither Jews nor Christians needed a formal promulgation of a listing of acceptable writings. The decisions at Jamnia and Trent were occasioned by internal strife, but controversy is not the only criterion; the role of the community is essential. Isolated individuals did not decide such matters on their own but in response to the call of the faith community's legitimate authority structure. The community (not the Bible) resolved the controversy — a dynamic still operative today.

When the Protestant Reformers changed the canon of the Bible, they had to take another step first, in order to legitimize their action: They had to attack the authority of the Church and replace it with their own authority. Clearly, however, no one can deny the authority and inspiration of the Church in relation to Scripture without also denying the inspiration of the Bible itself. Except for the authority of the Church, the non-canonical Gospel of Thomas (or any other writing purporting to tell "the Jesus story") could have claimed as much validity and canonicity as the Gospel of Matthew. The Bible's validity rests on the validity of the Church as authentic interpreter of Divine Revelation.

An examination of Scripture and Tradition demonstrates the interrelatedness and interdependence they have with each other and with the Church. Some critics accuse the Church of manipulating or altering the Scriptures, but nothing could be further from the truth. The Word of God can never be stagnant; rather, it must always be vibrant and alive for God's People. The Church does not change Scripture, but she does help her people grow in their understanding and ability to interpret God's Word. Just as the Holy Spirit brought new insights regarding the Lord's words to His apostles after His Death and Resurrection, so too does the same Spirit illuminate truths for Christ's brothers and sisters in His Church today.

In all of this, two extremes need to be avoided. The first deifies the Bible, while the second nearly denies it. People who subscribe to the first position must remember that the Chosen People existed without their Scriptures for centuries, and the Church existed without any New Testament writings for close to a generation and with no definitive canon for more than a century. The Church is the mother of the New Testament and the custodian of the Scriptures; her fidelity to the Lord is likewise judged by them. Sometimes we hear people say that one need not study history or philosophy or linguistics — just the Bible. This is a most narrow view. If it is correct that all truth is one, then even an apparently secular insight gained adds in some way to a deeper understanding of God's Word. That is what Matthew Arnold meant in *Culture and Anarchy* when he said: "No man who knows nothing else knows even his Bible."

The second group must recall that the Scriptures are a divine gift to be prayed with, reflected on, and used. As the Fathers of Vatican II put it: "The Church has always venerated the divine Scriptures as she venerates the Body of the Lord."[5] It is important, then, for Christians to be informed and formed by the Sacred Scriptures. In the Middle Ages, the Church showed her love for the Scriptures by chaining the Bible to library lecterns — not so that it would never be read but so that this precious book, meant to be available to all,

31

would not be stolen. In this way, the Bible would be available to all as a source of life and hope. Contemporary Christians should develop a similar reverence for the Scriptures, but a practical reverence shown forth in daily prayer and in study of the sacred texts. (Cf. CCC nn. 103, 131-133.)

A truly Catholic view of revelation takes all these seriously: God, the Church, the Church's Tradition, and the Church's Scriptures. The focus of our attention, however, is not the Church, the Scriptures, or Tradition, but God. The other three are means given to us to arrive at our end — union with God. (Cf. CCC n. 95.)

2

What Must I Do to Be Saved?

"N o one can see the reign of God unless he is begotten from above" (Jn 3:3).[1] On this point Catholics and Fundamentalists agree. "You must accept Jesus as your personal Savior," the TV evangelist declares. Here again Catholics and Fundamentalists are in agreement. In both areas, however, the words used mean very different things to the different parties involved. To clear up the misunderstanding, it will be necessary to explain what Catholics mean when they speak of being "born again" and of "accepting Jesus as one's personal Savior."

In answer to the question of when he was saved, one bishop replied that it happened some two thousand years ago on a hill outside of Jerusalem on a spring afternoon. He wasn't trying to be cute or clever; he was accurately reflecting the teaching of the Church: that the salvation of the world was sealed by Christ's Death on the cross. That was God's action (in Christ), but it requires a human response. The Hebrews were made the recipients of divine election by being formed into the Chosen People. However, they had to live by the covenant established between them and God. In the same way, the Death of Jesus brought about a new covenant in His blood, calling for a personal response.

The individual's response comes about through the operation of grace and by the action of the Church. God has placed within the human heart a desire for union with Him because God "wants all men to be saved and come to know the truth" (1 Tim 2:4). When confronted with the offer of salvation, a person is given the impulse to respond with faith, which is always a gift and always an act of the whole person. When we speak of faith as a gift, we mean that no human being can do anything to merit it but that it is freely bestowed by a gracious God. To be a fully human response, the act of faith must include both the intellect and the will. While it is correct to say that faith requires a risk or a leap, one must also add that it is not a blind leap but a reasoned one, for an act of faith devoid of reason is a less-than-human act, since it fails to include an essential element of the human person. (Cf. CCC nn. 74, 153-165, 183.)

Having been presented with the gift of faith, the person is then incorporated into Christ through Baptism, that sacrament which frees us from the sin of our first parents, inserts us into the Lord's Paschal Mystery, and makes us members of His Body, the Church. It is important to notice the presence of the Church throughout the process of salvation. (Cf. CCC nn. 166-169.)

While most Fundamentalists would agree with the broad outline of this presentation, they would take serious exception to several aspects. Many would balk at the notion of a "reasoned" leap of faith, but to despise reason is to despise the uniqueness of man, the very crown of creation that the Lord God found to be "very good" (Gen 1:31).

Although Fundamentalists recognize the need for Baptism, they frequently shy away from identifying the action as a sacrament or as a work of the Church. One can quibble about terminology, but the reality of the sacred action and its source in the community of the Church is beyond dispute. The effects of the sacrament are likewise beyond dispute: the removal of original sin (cf. Rom 5:12-19), participation in the Lord's Death and Resurrection (cf. Rom 6:3-5), and membership in the Church as a recognizable and real community (cf. 1 Cor 12:12f). (Cf. CCC n. 1213.)

The real controversy develops, however, when one entertains the prospect of infant Baptism. Fundamentalists seem so highly committed to the human response that they nearly eclipse the divine initiative. Infant Baptism emphasizes the fact that Almighty God is sovereign and can call whomever He wills. Birth from a Jewish mother makes one a Jew by that very fact, and thus a member of the Chosen People. Birth to a Christian family similarly makes a child eligible for membership in the people of the New Covenant. Christian parents, having given their child the gift of life, logically share with the child the gift of faith. And God, Who is no respecter of persons (cf. Acts 10:34), offers to the child the gift of eternal life through the saving waters of Baptism. The practice of infant Baptism is attested to implicitly in New Testament passages that speak of whole households (cf. Acts 16:15, 33) being received into the Church. Nowhere do we read that children were excluded from the process, perhaps because the apostolic Church knew what the Lord Jesus thought about such behavior (cf. Mk 10:14). (Cf. CCC nn. 1246, 1250-1252.)

Of course, faith is necessary for any Baptism — even that of an infant — but in this case, it is a faith that is "borrowed," since at some future moment that faith will have to be personally affirmed. For Catholics, this is traditionally done in the Sacrament of Confirmation, by which a Christian makes his own the faith he has received and is sealed with the Holy Spirit (cf. Acts 8:14-17). Confirmation continues the initiation process of a Christian, a process that finds its culmination in the Eucharist, as the believer is fed with the Bread of Life. (Cf. CCC nn. 1253, 1285, 1322.)

Having become a Christian, the believer must then live like one, and that is where good works find their place. It has been said that one is not reborn *by* good works but *to* good works, and that is very true. Because one has received the gift of new life in Christ, he or she must give evidence of a lively faith by a godly life, especially by attending to the needs of the poor and the oppressed (cf. Mt 25:31-46). This style of life is not an attempt to curry favor with God, but is a response of love and a powerful witness to the grace of election. For a devout Christian, there can never be any opposition between faith and works, for the first necessarily leads to the second. The Epistle of James has given classical expression to this insight: "What good is it to profess faith without practicing it? Such faith has no power to save one, has it? . . . Faith without works is as dead as a body without breath" (2:14, 26). In many ways the classical controversy over faith and works has been happily resolved by the Lutheran-Catholic accord of 1999 on this topic as both sides stressed the centrality of God's grace as the moving force behind either faith or works. (Cf. CCC nn. 1996, 2001.)

Once a person is saved, whether as an infant or an adult, that person cannot be a rugged individualist. Christianity is, by its very nature, a communal affair, which is to say an "ecclesial," or "churchly," reality. Contrary to what many Fundamentalists allege, the Church enhances a believer's relationship with Christ; the Church is a mediating structure and not an impediment. The scriptural data is eminently clear, namely, that Jesus intended a true and visible community to come into being. In Matthew 16 the reader finds Jesus informing Peter of the establishment of this Church, against which the gates of hell shall not prevail (cf. Mt 16:18). This passage cannot be interpreted in a purely spiritual sense, since Jesus instructs His disciples at a later point in that Gospel to refer earthly disputes to the same Church (cf. Mt 18:17). Hence, it is evident that Christ envisioned the formation of a visible structure here on earth. (Cf. CCC nn. 758-780.)

What is the precise role of the Church, according to the Scriptures? The community of the redeemed is to be a voice of witness (cf. Acts 1:8), a proclaimer of the coming kingdom (cf. Mt 10:7), and a liturgical assembly (cf. Acts 2:42), especially for the Eucharist (cf. Lk 22:19), until the Lord's Second Coming (cf. 1 Cor 11:26).

The Anglican theologian and archbishop William Temple once remarked that "the Church exists for those who are not yet members of her." In other words, the Church is to be a body of believers that is "mission-minded." Having received the Gospel message themselves, Christians need to share that message with others by offering them "the words of life" (1 Jn 1:1), in the hope that "the world may believe" (Jn 17:21). Faith is to be shared, but how? Not merely as individuals, but as a community. The evangelist says the world will believe not because of convincing argumentation or cleverly worded polemics but because of the unity of believers in Christ.

Our Lord makes this intention the focus of His high priestly prayer at the Last Supper: "I pray that they may be one in us, that the world may believe that you sent me" (Jn 17:21). A united witness is required, and never fragmented or divisive efforts. Repeatedly, Jesus bade His followers to proclaim the kingdom. God's kingdom is both a present and a future reality, something "already" but also "not yet." St. Luke tells us, "The reign of God is already in your midst" (17:21).

The kingdom takes root in an individual when the Word is heard, received, and lived. But sin in the world keeps the kingdom at bay (therefore, "Thy kingdom come"), calling for a counterforce: grace in the world. The grace of God is made visible by the kingdom life of the Church, which exhibits aspects of both the "already" and the "not yet." (Cf. CCC nn. 849-856.)

The sinless Church anticipates the kingdom in the liturgy, while the incomplete nature of the kingdom is highlighted by the presence of still-sinful members within that Church.

The Church is "a royal priesthood" (1 Pt 2:9), that is, a liturgical people. Private prayer is, of course, necessary; however, the New Testament is replete with examples of the apostolic community engaged in communal worship. The most significant of these prayer forms is the celebration of the Holy Eucharist. This communal celebration actively recalls the saving Death and Resurrection of the Lord Jesus Christ. The Eucharist is of absolute importance in the life of the Church, since it was instituted by Christ Himself at the Last Supper, where He commanded His followers to do what He had done in remembrance of Him (cf. Lk 22:19). This command was not limited to the apostles, for St. Paul tells us that we must witness to Jesus' Death in the Eucharist "until he comes" (1 Cor 11:26). Thus, the Church must preach the good news of Jesus Christ and witness to His Death and Resurrection in the Eucharist until His Second Coming. (Cf. CCC nn. 1546-1547.)

Far from being a mere collection of individuals, the Church on earth possesses an essential unity due to her relationship with her Founder, Jesus Christ. The Church is, as St. Paul's theology depicts it, the Body of Christ (cf. Col 1:24). Paul is not speaking solely in a metaphorical sense, since he explains to the Church at Corinth that their "bodies are members of Christ" (1 Cor 6:15). Therefore, there is something mystical associated with the Body of Christ, as the body of believers interacts in a special way with each other and the transcendent Savior Who is its Head. (Cf. CCC nn. 813-822.)

The unity and cohesiveness of the Body of Christ goes beyond the human unity that a community of believers may possess. In a very real sense, the body of believers (the Church) shares a common life — members and Head together. As St. Paul said, "Since one died for all, all died" (2 Cor 5:14). The members of the Body of Christ have died with Him, so that one day they may share in His Resurrection. (Cf. CCC nn. 775-776.)

This oneness exists not only between the Body and its Head, but also among the members of the Body themselves. St. Paul tells us: "If one member suffers, all suffer together; if one member is honored, all rejoice together" (1 Cor 12:26). The Body of Christ, while comprised of numerous individuals, possesses a supreme unity of spirit and purpose that cannot be broken. And it is the Holy Spirit that secures and seals this unity, since, as Paul tells us, "it was in one Spirit that all of us . . . were baptized into one body" (1 Cor 12:13). (Cf. CCC n. 792.)

In his Letter to the Ephesians, St. Paul further emphasizes the intrinsic unity of Christ and His Church by portraying the Church as the Bride of Christ (cf. Eph 5:22f). He explains that Christ gave "himself up for her to make her holy" and encourages husbands and wives to love each other as Christ loved the Church. In man's attempt to explain the relationship between the Lord and His Church, no better analogy could be found than that of the marital union in which "the two shall be made into one" (Eph 5:31). For his part, St. Paul does not merely hint at the analogy but states clearly that "it refers to Christ and the church" (Eph 5:32). In view of the impossibility of separating Christ from His Church, a theology that rejects the need for the Church is scripturally misguided at best and spiritually dangerous at worst. (Cf. CCC nn. 796, 817-819.)

The spiritual union of the Church with Christ grows by means of the sacraments. Through Baptism, we share in the atoning Death of Jesus Christ. We enter into a personal relationship with our Savior and into membership in the Church, which is His Body.

This awareness is heightened by means of the other sacraments, particularly the Eucharist. It has already been noted that the Church is to celebrate the Eucharist in remembrance of Christ until He comes again. The Eucharist, however, does far more than bear witness to Christ's salvific Death. It allows the members of Christ's Body to share in that Death and to move into a more perfect union with one another, through the Lord Jesus Christ. St. Paul explained this phenomenon concisely: "Is not the cup of blessing we bless a sharing in the blood of Christ? And is not the bread we break a sharing in the body of Christ? Because the loaf of bread is one, we many though we are, are one body, for we all partake of the one loaf" (1 Cor 10:16f). Is it an accident that Christian communities that are not eucharistically oriented have such difficulty living in unity? When people share a common faith, their incipient unity is fed by the Eucharist and becomes an ever-deepening reality and a powerful sign to the world. The sign of the Eucharist makes the whole People of God into a sign. Conversely, a failure to celebrate the Eucharist regularly is a denial to oneself and one's community of the source of Christian unity. (Cf. CCC n. 1325.)

The individual Christian, while having a personal relationship with God, is also bound to God in and through the community of believers, the Church. Not only may one not separate oneself from the Body of Christ any more than from its Head, but it is the duty of each Christian to help the Body to flourish, to build up the Church. St. Paul exhorts the Christians at Corinth to be rich in those spiritual gifts "that build up the church" (1 Cor 14:12), and his teaching is no less pertinent today.

Traditionally, Catholics emphasize the communal dimension of a life of faith while Protestants have stressed the individual or impersonal. Neither is wrong; both are needed, and Catholicism acknowledges this fact. Personal prayer is an essential part of a Catholic's life, taking on a variety of forms, including spontaneous prayer, meditation, reading of Scripture, and formal prayers (like the Rosary).

Three Catholic devotions, however, are powerful statements of the Church's concern for her sons and daughters to have a personal relationship with God. Worship of the Eucharistic Christ, especially through services outside the celebration of Mass, stresses the fact that Christ died for us as individuals and is today available to us as individuals and not simply as part of an anonymous group. The one-on-one dimension comes across as the individual speaks to the Eucharistic Lord and awaits His response. This love is crystallized in the devotion to the Sacred Heart of Jesus, whose most obvious scriptural origins are found in John's account of the wounding of the Lord's Sacred Heart in His saving Death on the cross (cf. Jn 19:34); indeed, every passage that speaks of Christ's love for us provides a scriptural basis for this devotion. Catholics observe Fridays as days of special penance to identify with their suffering Lord, responding to love with love. But Christians, even the devout, still suffer the effects of a fallen nature; therefore, they sin. When they sin, Catholics avail themselves of Christ's mercy in the Sacrament of Penance. In a personal encounter with Jesus (through the person of the priest), the sinner confesses his sins, expresses

41

sorrow, and hears the Lord's consoling words of forgiveness, bringing with them the experience of reconciliation and peace. (Cf. CCC nn. 1378, 2669, 1422-1470.)

Many other Catholic traditions could be cited, but the point should be clear by now that Catholics do see the need for a personal relationship with God and that they have it. Our view is that personal prayer brings life to communal prayer, and that communal worship plunges the believer more deeply into the Lord's life so that the personal relationship is indeed fostered.

The critical question in all this talk about salvation, however, comes down to this: "How do I know I am saved?" No absolute assurance is available; one must have recourse to the virtue of hope, which is a firm trust in God's goodness and love. Some Fundamentalists hold that someone who is saved "knows" for sure. St. Paul had some different ideas on the subject. He said that the Philippians needed to "work with anxious concern to achieve [their] salvation" (2:12). Many Protestant translations actually speak of working out one's salvation "in fear and trembling." Paul likewise warned against presumption in this matter by reminding the Corinthians: "Let anyone who thinks he is standing upright watch out lest he fall!" (1 Cor 10:12). No, we are saved in hope. We believe that God has given us the means to be saved and that, with His grace and assistance, we will respond in such a way that the salvation Christ earned for us on Calvary will indeed be credited to us as righteousness (cf. Rom 4). (Cf. CCC nn. 1817-1821.)

Evangelist Jimmy Swaggart has stated that "once individuals are saved — if they are Catholic — they should 'come out from among them and be separate.' "[2] He labels Catholicism a false religion and indicates that the Church will only hinder an individual's personal relationship with God. Such an image of the Church, however, overlooks her very nature and mission, as well as the vital role she plays in guiding the People of God toward salvation. Swaggart's advice is that "every Christian should find a good Bible-based, Bible-preaching, soul-winning Church where the Holy Spirit prevails."[3] He is absolutely correct. What he fails to realize, however, is that Catholics have already found such a Church.

3

Is the
Catholic Church
Christian?

The title of this chapter is no accident; indeed, it goes to the very heart of the matter. It is interesting to note two points in this regard. First, although the Catholic Church has many theological differences with other religious bodies, she is very hesitant about denying Christian status to those who claim it for themselves, as long as certain basic criteria are met (e.g., belief in the Holy Trinity and the divinity of Christ). The reason for this posture of the Church, however, is the second point that needs to be raised. In presenting the Catholic Faith, the Church never contrasts her theology with that of other Christian bodies. She does not engage in diatribe, much less "sheep-stealing." Why so? Because she is confident of her position and has no need to define herself in terms of other groups. The truth of the Catholic Faith and the witness of history are sufficient validation. (Cf. CCC n. 819.)

Conversely, so many Fundamentalist preachers spend most of their time attacking Catholic doctrine and practice, leading one to wonder if their goal is to bring people to Christ or to move Catholics out of the Church. Of course, they hold that the second goal must be achieved before the first can be realized. Close examination of their approach, however, demonstrates their own basic insecurity — since, if they are intelligent people, they know that their attacks on the Church cannot stand up scripturally, theologically, historically, or sociologically. The very fact that they need to mention Catholicism is an implicit acknowledgment of their indebtedness to the Church; after all, Buddhists do not teach their faith by referring to Catholicism, for there is no necessary link. No Christian body, though, can avoid reference to the Catholic Church, since she is, as Vatican II reaffirmed, the Church of Christ.[1] (Cf. CCC n. 816.)

Some of the charges leveled against the Church by Fundamentalists are based on ignorance; some are humorous; others are just mean-spirited. Nevertheless, I would like to take them all seriously and respond to them with honesty and with charity. Let me present them as a series of Fundamentalist propositions.

The word "Catholic" is never used of the Church in Scriptures. True, but what is the import of that? The New Testament never uses the word "Trinity" either, yet no self-respecting Christian would hesitate to do so; in fact, it is an essential part of the Christian vocabulary. No, we must learn to distinguish between words on the one hand and concepts or realities on the other. Simply because a particular word is not used does not automatically mean that a concept is not believed. (Cf. CCC nn. 830-831.)

The clear, unmistakable evidence of the Scriptures indicates that Our Lord did indeed establish a Church (cf. Mt 16:18), which He intended to spread to the very ends of the earth (cf. Mt 28:19f). That is, His Church was to be a universal body, encompassing the whole of humanity, which is precisely the meaning of "catholic."

The Catholic Church did not exist for the first three centuries of the Christian era but was a political creation of Constantine. Such an allegation cannot be squared with the facts of history. At this juncture, it is well to part company with church historians (who might be accused of bias) and to seek out the evaluation of secular historians. Not a single history of Western civilization can be found that does not present the Catholic Church as the undisputed mother of Christianity, from whom every other Christian body descends.[2] Even main-line Protestant denominations admit their roots to be in Catholicism; they would say their break with Rome was necessary for a variety of reasons, but they would never deny their original source of Christian faith.

Undoubtedly, Constantine (like secular rulers before and after him) saw political potential in having a unified faith among those he governed, but Constantine did not create the Church; he inherited it. While the Church must always be careful of political alliances, she cannot avoid all contact with the world, as the New Testament makes abundantly clear (cf. Mt 22:21; 1 Tim 2:1-3). (Cf. CCC nn. 1897-1904, 2244-2246.)

Catholicism is not a Christian religion because it makes use of pagan customs. Like the Israelites despoiling the Egyptians and Paul trying to find common ground with the Athenians, the Church has never despised the good in human culture. Whatever is good — even in paganism — can and should be incorporated into Christian life and practice so as to enrich our faith and to make converts realize that so much of their former way of life was a true preparation for the Gospel message.

The Church has "baptized" many pagan customs, just as she has baptized many pagans. The critical point is that

47

once the process has taken place, the matter under consideration can no longer be considered pagan, since they have been given over to Christ.

The Church took the pagan feast of *Sol Invictus* ("The Unconquered Sun") and gave Christians an opportunity to celebrate at the same time as their pagan neighbors a feast of their own: the birth, not of the Sun God, but of the Son of God. Hence, our Christmas festivities, which few Fundamentalists question and usually enthusiastically celebrate.

The Church found herself living in a highly organized Roman Empire and decided to use that structure for the spread of the Gospel. Thus, the establishment of dioceses as regional divisions of the universal Church, designed to facilitate communication among the local churches and to preserve the unity of the Church.

Dozens of similar examples could be cited. A knee-jerk, negative reaction to secular culture has never characterized Christianity from the earliest days. The apostolic Church endeavored to make the Faith as palatable as possible and to minimize unnecessary burdens for pagan converts (cf. Acts 15:28), a pattern and mode of thought accepted by the Church in every successive generation.

The Roman Catholic "system" is taught nowhere in the Bible. By the word "system," critics usually have in mind practices like prayers for the dead, the use of statues and images, the institution of the papacy. Many of the traditions so offensive to some Fundamentalists do have biblical foundation; others are there in seminal form; still others are not found in the Bible but are in harmony with it.

The Bible cannot be treated like a big dictionary, which one consults expecting to find a solution to every problem in every detail. As already indicated in Chapter 1, we Catholics

48

reject the view that the Bible is the only source of Divine Revelation; God also reveals His will to us through His Son's Church. Therefore, the silence of Scripture on many matters enables the Church to opt for that freedom of the children of God, praised by St. Paul (cf. Rom 8:21).

The sacraments cannot be found in the New Testament. Such an assertion is shocking to any serious Scripture scholar. The Church has declared the sacraments to be seven in number; while the form of the sacraments has changed many times over the centuries, the essence of them has not, so that we believe if Jesus were to enter a Catholic church today, He would certainly recognize the rites being celebrated. (Cf. CCC nn. 1113-1116.)

John the Evangelist locates the source of sacramental life in the Church in Christ's redeeming Death on the cross, as we learn that from the Lord's wounded side flowed blood and water, symbols of the Eucharist and Baptism. Christians for two millennia have never questioned the divine institution of sacraments. While the Protestant reformers quibbled over this rite or that, they never doubted the importance of a sacramental life for Christians as means of establishing and maintaining contact with the Risen Lord.

Each and every sacrament can be demonstrated as having multiple scriptural warranties. Let one or two suffice for each, for the sake of brevity: Baptism (Mt 28:19); Confirmation (Acts 8:14f); Penance (Jn 20:23); Eucharist (Mt 26:26-28; Mk 14:22-24; Lk 22:19f; Jn 6); Matrimony (Eph 5:30-32); Holy Orders (2 Tim 1:6); Anointing of the Sick (James 5:14).

The enjoining of abstinence is condemned in 1 Timothy 4:1-3. When the Church urges her sons and daughters to abstain from certain foods on special days or even from sexual relations (as do clergy and Religious for the sake of the kingdom), she is doing so not to suggest that such things are bad but to affirm their basic goodness and to remind Christians that there is a yet higher good, which should be sought. Fasting and abstaining are means traditionally used in Judaism and Christianity to gain control over one's senses in an effort to dispose the believer to union with the Almighty. Such mortifications are also intended as penance for sin, which Our Lord Himself indicated His disciples would do after His departure from their midst (Mt 9:15). (Cf. CCC nn. 2043, 1434, 1579.)

The Church has always been the enemy of Bible-reading on the part of Christians. This is patently false. In every century the Church has produced Scripture scholars who have devoted their lives to the study and teaching of the Sacred Scriptures. Vernacular translations of the Bible were done with care and caution, yes, to ensure the integrity of the Word of God. Illiterate peasants were not given the Bible, of course; to what good, since they could not read? Nevertheless, Bible history was taught; church windows told the story of the Bible in art; Scripture reading has always been an essential part of every Mass; Scripture quotations or paraphrases form the heart of all liturgical prayer. (Cf. CCC nn. 131-133.)

What the Church has always discouraged is an individualistic approach to Bible-reading that removes the Scriptures from their source in the Church. To hold that an individual Christian can have a deeper insight into the meaning of a biblical text than the entire Body of Christ over the centuries is tantamount to spiritual pride of the worst sort. Now that the members of the Church are better educated, the Church actively encourages her sons and daughters to read and pray over the Scriptures, wherein all find life.

Contrary to Galatians 1:8f, many Catholics believe new revelations to be on the horizon. Once again, such an impression is based on misunderstanding. Catholics seek no new revelations; we believe that everything necessary for man's salvation has been revealed in Jesus Christ. Any new or personal or private revelations are always judged by the Church against the background of the unchanging basic message of the Gospel. Apparitions of Our Lord, Our Lady, or the other saints — accepted by the Church as valid — have been nothing but restatements of the core of the Gospel. The message of Fátima could be best summarized as, "Reform your lives and believe in the Gospel" (Mk 1:15). (Cf. CCC nn. 66-67.)

Revelation 17 cursed the Church as the great whore of Babylon. Scripturally speaking, this interpretation is indefensible; it is eminently clear that the "whore of Revelation" is the pagan city of Rome, which was responsible for the blood of the early Christian martyrs.

While individuals in the Church have been sinners (and always will be), the Church herself as the Bride of Christ is sinless and immaculate (cf. Eph 5:27), producing holy children for the heavenly Father in every age. It is no coincidence that the sons and daughters of the Church have brought forth the greatest works of literature, art, and music over two thousand years. Jesus said, "You will know them by their fruits" (Mt 7:20). It is no whore but a loving, kindly, faithful Mother who has ever had such progeny. (Cf. CCC nn. 823-829.)

Catholicism binds its members to doctrines not taught in the Word of God. Not all the teachings of the Church are of equal value or of equally binding force. The Second Vatican Council observed that there exists a "hierarchy of truths,"[3] so that the use of Latin in the liturgy, Friday abstinence, clerical celibacy, and even certain Marian devotions do not have the same force as the doctrines of the Trinity, Christ's redemptive sacrifice, or the Resurrection. (Cf. CCC nn. 82, 90.)

This distinction is critical, since it separates essentials from non-essentials. The Church has always been able to do this, while many of her critics have not.

The Catholic Church is constantly inventing new dogmas. The Church does not "invent" dogmas but "defines" them. Fundamentalists are often fond of asserting that the Church came up with the doctrine of Mary's Assumption nineteen hundred years after the fact. This shows confusion about the process of dogmatic definition. (Cf. CCC nn. 88, 95.)

From earliest times, Christians have believed that Our Lady shared in her Son's Resurrection immediately after her passing from this earthly life. In fact, one of the oldest churches in the Holy Land is that of Mary's Dormition, venerated as the site of Our Lady's "falling asleep" and assumption into heaven. This was thus always a part of the Faith of the Church. All that Pope Pius XII did in 1950 was to proclaim that the doctrine has always belonged to the Deposit of Faith, an action he took after consultation with all the bishops of the world and at their urging.

Simply because a doctrine was not defined for centuries does not mean it was not believed. To discover what is believed, a study of the Church's prayers and liturgy usually provides solid information. On the other hand, when a teaching is defined, this means that the doctrine in question is indeed contained in Divine Revelation and has always been believed. Therefore, the Church proposes no new doctrines for the faithful; anyone who doubts this need only look to the historical record to discover the continuity of the Christian Faith throughout the ages.

"Is the Catholic Church Christian?" By taking seriously all the possible objections to her Christianity, the reader can see in the responses that the Catholic Church is not only a Christian body but also possesses the very fullness of Christian truth. Indeed, her critics attain their identity only by subtracting from the fullness of her two-thousand-year-old message.

4

Who
Rules the
Church?

The bottom-line answer to this question is at once very simple and complex: Christ rules His Church, since He is her Founder and her Lord. Any who would exercise authority in the Church must do so as people answerable to the Lord. Few would doubt the need for and legitimacy of a hierarchy (sacred authority system), because Jesus made it abundantly clear that His Church should have such a structure; what He did castigate was a worldly style of government for this sacred society, based on a desire for power rather than service (cf. Lk 22:25f). (Cf. CCC nn. 874-875.)

Honesty requires one to admit that there have been abuses of ecclesiastical authority over the centuries, but this fact alone does not invalidate the basic correctness of the concept, any more than the fact of adultery invalidates the notion of permanent and exclusive commitments in marriage. The more logical and mature approach seeks to uncover the original intent and structure of authority in the Church.

Doctrines regarding apostolic succession, Petrine primacy, and papal infallibility have often been the focus of Fundamentalist criticism, but a clear understanding of the precise teachings of the Church on these matters is often lacking. The

Church sees her teaching authority (Magisterium) as a service rendered to the People of God in fulfillment of the Lord's commission to the apostles to spread the Gospel to the very ends of the earth. Furthermore, it is important to recall that the Church forces her rule on no one, for membership in the Church is exclusively on the basis of free association.

The Catholic Church refers to herself as "holy" and "apostolic," by which designations she wishes to explain her present identity in terms of her origins. The Church is holy, in spite of the presence of sinners in her midst, because Jesus Christ her Founder is holy and because she has produced holy members in every age. The Church is apostolic because she is built on the foundation of the apostles (cf. Eph 2:20) and to this day professes the apostolic Faith. Catholics believe that the bishops are the successors of the apostles. The doctrine of apostolic succession was explained at the Second Vatican Council in this way: "Bishops have by divine institution taken the place of the apostles as pastors of the Church." Or, again: "The apostolic tradition is manifested and preserved in the whole world by those who were made bishops by the apostles and their successors down to our own time."[1] (Cf. CCC nn. 823-829, 857-865.)

This doctrine, however, is not a creation of twentieth-century theologians but has been a constant feature of Catholic life since the time of the apostles, with ample scriptural support, as well as historical reliability. In the very moment when Jesus commissioned the apostles to teach and make disciples of all nations, He likewise gave them the promise of His presence and assistance to accomplish the task (cf. Mt 28:20). Since God is always faithful to His promises, one can be certain that Christ's guarantee of His presence did not die with the last apostle, for the Lord had promised never to leave His people orphaned (cf. Jn 14:18).

Authority in the Church exists to safeguard the integrity of the Gospel message and to foster the unity of the Church. That the apostles chose successors for themselves is clearly attested to throughout the New Testament, but most especially in the Pastoral Epistles. Since the question of bishops and priests will be treated in Chapter 5, a detailed discussion here is not needed. Let the reader note, however, at the end of this section some of the scriptural passages that document this development[2] and demonstrate beyond the shadow of a doubt that the apostolic Church saw the need for the transmission of authority to a new generation as something willed by Jesus for His Church (cf. Acts 1:15-26).

Although many Protestants question the doctrine of apostolic succession, the debate on this principle is not nearly as great as the criticism of Catholic teaching regarding the primacy of the apostle Peter. Fundamentalists usually charge that there is no record that Peter held any venerable position within the Church. If we examine the role of Peter in the New Testament, however, we find significant evidence that directly contradicts this assertion. (Cf. CCC nn. 552-556.)

Perhaps the most frequently quoted passage regarding Petrine supremacy in the New Testament is Matthew 16:17-19. (Cf. CCC nn. 440-443.) In it, Jesus renames Simon (Peter) and He entrusts to him the keys to the kingdom of heaven. Why this honor? Peter has just proclaimed Jesus to be the Messiah, a revelation that comes, as Jesus tells us, from His heavenly Father (cf. Mt 16:17). (Cf. CCC nn. 880-882.)

Thus it is upon Peter himself that Jesus will build His Church. Fundamentalists will counter that the keys given to Peter merely "provide access," as do keys in the physical sense. This simplistic view, however, overlooks two important points: Peter was given the keys of the kingdom singularly and was entrusted with them in conjunction with the powers of binding and loosing. In rabbinic terms (which is the only correct way to interpret so Jewish a Gospel as Matthew), the ability to bind and loose is equated with the authority to decide what is allowed and forbidden by Law. Binding and loosing also have an alternate meaning, denoting the authority to include persons in the community or to exclude or excommunicate them. Thus, Peter was being granted a special role by Christ related to the teaching and life of the community.[3] (Cf. CCC nn. 981-983.)

This passage of Scripture, so controverted for centuries and proudly emblazoned in the dome of St. Peter's Basilica in Rome, is not the only place in the New Testament that shows Peter in a different light from the rest of the apostles. In fact, several other pericopes (sacred texts) might be even more convincing. The sum total of such passages is so overwhelming that one wonders how someone cannot see the case clearly. Some years ago an ecumenical team of scholars researched this question in an honest and objective fashion; their conclusions are of great significance and shall be summarized in what follows.[4]

The writers of the New Testament gave to Peter a variety of titles with some powerful imagery behind them. He was the great Christian fisherman, singled out in Luke 5:10. John 21 shows him to be both shepherd and martyr, giving his life for his flock in imitation of the Savior. Peter is presented as the confessor of the true Faith (cf. Mt 16), as well as its guardian (cf. 2 Pt). He was the recipient of special revelations and also the initiator of a course of action as a result: the Messiahship of Jesus (Mt 16:17); the experience of the Transfiguration (Mt 17:4; Mk 9:5; Lk 9:33); the Ananias and Sapphira episode (Acts 5); the vision regarding Cornelius (Acts 10); the miraculous release from prison (Acts 12:7-11).

What other data can be gleaned from the Scriptures

regarding Peter? Christ's renaming of him "stuck," as he is consistently called "Cephas," the Aramaic word for Peter, or "rock" (e.g., Mk 3:17; Mt 16:18; Jn 1:42). He figured prominently in post-Resurrection appearances of Our Lord, and his testimony was considered a validating element for others' encounters with the Risen Christ (cf. 1 Cor 15:5; Lk 24:34; Mk 16:7). He was the most important of the Twelve, always first in apostolic lists. His missionary career is beyond dispute, and he appears to have been a theological moderate between James and Paul. Finally, he was a weak sinner who was called Satan by Jesus and accused by the Lord of having little faith; he proved his weakness by his threefold denial of Christ. (Cf. CCC n. 642.)

This is an impressive pulling together of texts, especially when one realizes that no other leader of the early Church is accorded such attention in the Scriptures. Two other passages require special analysis.

In Luke, Jesus tells Peter that Satan has asked for the disciples, that he may sift them all like wheat (cf. Lk 22:31). Jesus comments, however, that He has prayed that Peter's faith may never fail. It is significant that Jesus prays for Peter alone and commissions him to care for the other disciples: "You in turn must strengthen your brothers" (Lk 22:32). Luke accords Peter a place among, yet apart from and above, the other apostles. (Cf. CCC n. 552.)

If Luke can be said to introduce the special role played by Peter among the apostles, then this introduction is refined and clarified in the Gospel of John. In John 21:15-17, the Risen Christ asks Peter three times if he loves Him. Peter responds affirmatively in each instance and is given three injunctions by Christ: "Feed my lambs"; "Tend my sheep"; "Feed my sheep." These commands provide a clear analogy between the roles of Christ and Peter with respect to the

Church. John tells us that Jesus is the Good Shepherd caring for His flock (cf. Jn 10:11-16). We also know from Luke's Gospel that Christ's followers are the flock cared for by the Good Shepherd (cf. Lk 12:32). Thus, by instructing Peter to tend and feed His sheep, Christ was designating Peter as the shepherd of His flock on earth. (Cf. CCC n. 552.)

It is also important to note that Peter is asked to proclaim his love for the Lord three times, clearly (and painfully) harking back to Peter's triple denial of Christ before His crucifixion. Peter is given the opportunity to rehabilitate himself, does so to Jesus' satisfaction, and is subsequently charged to tend Christ's flock and to nurture His people.

For those who are fond of pointing out the sinfulness of ecclesiastical leaders, past and present, it is good to underscore the fact that this mission to Peter is given to him in the very context of Christ's reminding him that he has sinned.

Having demonstrated the special role of Peter in the New Testament, one must now move a step further to the question of papal infallibility. The charism of infallibility is that gift whereby the Holy Spirit preserves the Church in the truth of the apostolic Faith. The Fathers of the First Vatican Council saw infallibility as the means by which "the whole flock of Christ might be kept away from the poison of error and be nourished by the food of heavenly doctrine."[5] To speak of "papal infallibility," then, is to identify only one aspect of infallibility, which is a gift to the whole Church, for the sake of the whole Church. The charism of infallibility comes into play when the Pope, as head of the college of bishops, or the entire body of bishops (in union with the Pope) speak the faith of the Church. The Second Vatican Council expressed it thus:

> The Roman Pontiff, head of the college of bishops,
> enjoys this infallibility in virtue of his office, when, as

supreme pastor and teacher of all the faithful — who confirms his brethren in the Faith (cf. Lk 22:32) — he proclaims in an absolute decision a doctrine pertaining to faith or morals. . . . The infallibility promised to the Church is also present in the body of bishops when, together with Peter's successor, they exercise the supreme teaching office.[6]

What does this mean concretely? The Church teaches that the Pope is infallible when teaching on matters of faith and morals and authoritatively speaking *ex cathedra* ("from the chair" of Peter), as the vicar of Christ on earth. This is a very specific and limited power. People outside the Church sometimes have the impression that the Pope can pronounce infallibly on any topic he chooses. As is obvious from reading the official ecclesiastical documents cited above, this is not the case; infallible teaching is limited to faith and morals. Furthermore, neither the Pope nor an ecumenical council can "create" or "invent" new doctrines and propose them for belief. An infallible dogmatic definition means that the particular doctrine at issue has always been taught and believed but that this is now being said formally and solemnly. (Cf. CCC nn. 889-892.)

Some critics of papal primacy argue that the See of Rome has no legitimate claim to authority because Peter was never in Rome; no serious historian — Protestant, Catholic, or secular — holds such a position, especially in the light of modern archeological discoveries. Others maintain that if there was a "primate" of sorts in the apostolic Church, it was James and not Peter; the scriptural data presented here is overwhelming in regard to Peter and scarcely available for James. Still others assert that papal authority was a medieval accretion or even an invention of the nineteenth century; let

Irenaeus writing in 202 serve as a witness: "For with this Church [Rome], all other churches must bring themselves into line, on account of its superior authority."[7] (Cf. CCC n. 834.)

The matter of infallibility must also be viewed from the perspective of the development of doctrine. Simply because a teaching was not officially affirmed until a certain time does not mean that the reality being taught did not exist, in fact, prior to an official pronouncement. Furthermore, it is not uncommon for the Church not to define dogmas (i.e., promulgate officially) when they are generally held. No definition of Christ's divinity existed until the Council of Nicaea in 325, not because the Church did not believe it but because the doctrine was not under serious attack and was generally believed. The same is true of papal infallibility. As the Church was buffeted by the storms of Rationalism in the nineteenth century, it became necessary to define certain teachings that had always been accepted and even taken for granted.

The doctrine of infallibility is derived from the principle of apostolic succession and from the fact that Jesus Christ promised His presence to the apostles when He sent them forth to teach all the nations (cf. Mt 28:20). The Pope and bishops are heirs to the first teaching commission of the Lord and, on that very account, also heirs to the promise of divine assistance. The Church has always held that God has revealed Himself to His people and will actively work to provide such revelation. Hence, the Church takes Jesus at His word when He says that the Holy Spirit "will instruct you in everything" (Jn 14:26; cf. Jn 16:13) and believes that the Holy Spirit will work through fallible men to ensure that the members of the Body of Christ are taught the infallible truth of Christ.

A final criticism of the Church centers upon the abuse of authority by some clerics in history, especially during the

Inquisition. While indefensible in practice, the Inquisition must be placed within its own intellectual, religious, and social milieu in order to be assessed fairly.[8] Although the Church would repudiate the excesses of the Inquisition today, one can no more use that aberration as a norm for defining Catholic doctrine than one could call for the dissolution of Protestant denominations because of persecutions carried out by them during the Reformation or the Salem witch trials. (Cf. CCC n. 853.)

Far from being repressive, authority and structure within the Church allow for continuity of doctrine and provide for freedom to preach the Gospel. As has already been noted, the teaching authority of the Church is a service rendered to God's People in fulfillment of Christ's commission to spread the Gospel. If the Church were to abdicate her responsibility in this area, not only would Christ's commission be carried out less effectively, but the essential unity of the Body of Christ would be irreparably harmed. Authority in the Church, then, is for service of Christ, His Gospel, and His People. (Cf. CCC nn. 874-879.)

5

Did Christ Establish the Priesthood?

One of the distinguishing features of Catholicism is its ministerial priesthood. The Church teaches that this is a sacrament, instituted by Christ, which commissions men to continue the Lord's ministry on earth, under the guidance of the Holy Spirit. Fundamentalists dispute this teaching, and some go as far as to claim that "the title and office of priest is [sic] empty and erroneous."[1] (Cf. CCC nn. 1546-1577.)

These critics are quite correct in saying that the New Testament is clear in describing the entire community of the Church as a "royal priesthood" (1 Pt 2:9). If so, why a priestly "caste" within the Church? The Hebrew Scriptures spoke of the Israelites as a royal priesthood (cf. Ex 19:6), but they still had a priestly class. If the Israelite community as a whole was to fulfill its priestly witness in the world, it needed the ministry of priests. The Church is no different: Having been ministered to by their priests, the Christian people can then minister to the world.

No competition should exist between clergy and laity because all Christians are called to serve both Christ and the world; it is not a question of who is better but merely of different ways to serve. A careful reflection on Paul's theology of the Church as the Body of Christ could be very profitable (cf. 1 Cor 12).

As Christ had promised to be with His Church until the end of time (cf. Mt 28:20), it was logical and necessary that Jesus' disciples would select men to succeed them in their ministry. Certainly, there is ample scriptural evidence to undergird this conclusion. In his Second Letter to Timothy, Paul reminds Timothy "to stir into flame the gift of God bestowed when my hands were laid on you" (2 Tim 1:6).[2] Timothy was commissioned to testify to the Lord by Paul and was imbued with the gift of God by the laying on of hands, a traditional practice that is the central rite of ordinations to this day.[3] It is evident that Timothy was selected to carry on the apostolic mission, since Paul later instructs Timothy himself to choose successors: "What you have heard from me before many witnesses entrust to faithful men who will be able to teach others also" (2 Tim 2:2). This is not merely an instruction to select followers, but a conferral of the right to ordain successors to the ministry.

St. Paul underlines the sacred and serious nature of this power in the caution he issues in his First Letter to Timothy: "Never lay hands hastily on anyone, or you may be sharing in the misdeeds of others" (1 Tim 5:22). If the laying on of hands were not a conferral of a sacred power, Paul would not have issued such grave words of warning. (Cf. CCC n. 1120.)

A call to service in the Church comes from God, but it is acknowledged and validated by the Church. No record exists in the New Testament or thereafter of any man declaring himself to be a Christian minister on his own authority. That is obviously the meaning of a passage like: "Do not trust every spirit, but put the spirits to a test to see if they belong to God, because many false prophets have appeared in the world"

(1 Jn 4:1). While goodwill should usually be presumed of self-proclaimed ministers, the Scriptures suggest that they be ignored unless it is clear they are "of the Spirit." The way they prove they are "of the Spirit" is by building up the Church (cf. 1 Cor 14:12). (Cf. CCC n. 1578.)

A priest is a witness to the Gospel and a proclaimer of that Gospel. That Word then needs to take on flesh (cf. Jn 1:14). Hence, a priest is ordained for two specific functions: to offer the Sacrifice of the Mass and to be an agent of reconciliation in the Sacrament of Penance. A priest must also do more than this: He must truly be a father to his people, standing as a constant sign of dedication to the Gospel and reflecting the compassion and mercy of Christ. (Cf. CCC nn. 1142, 1461-1467.)

The priesthood exists for the Eucharist; if there were no Eucharist, there would be no need of the priesthood. But fidelity to the Lord's command requires the continued celebration of the Eucharist, which, in turn, requires a ministerial priesthood. Some detailed analysis is necessary here.

As Jesus blessed the bread and wine at the Last Supper, He said: "This is my body to be given for you. . . . This cup is the new covenant in my blood, which will be shed for you" (Lk 22:19f). In this same passage, Jesus commanded the apostles to "do this as a remembrance of me." The Lord's followers were instructed to offer this sacrificial meal in remembrance of the first Eucharistic Celebrant, Jesus Christ. Thus are the sacraments of the Eucharist and Orders inextricably bound up with each other. (Cf. CCC nn. 1341-1377.)

In addition to the Catholic belief that Christ is truly present in the Eucharist (cf. Jn 6:53ff), the Church also teaches that Jesus Christ formed a New Covenant with His people through His own Passion, Death, and Resurrection. This Paschal Mystery is celebrated and renewed through the Eucharistic Sacrifice: "For this is my blood, the blood of the new covenant, to be poured out in behalf of many for the forgiveness of sins" (Mt 26:28). Jesus' words clearly hark back to those of Moses in Exodus when he ratified the Old Covenant with God (cf. Ex 24:8). The apostles, familiar with the Scriptures and with their own heritage, could not have missed the allusion to the ratification of the Old Covenant nor the importance that Jesus' words imparted to the Eucharistic meal and, therefore, to their own priestly ministries. (Cf. CCC nn. 1373-1377, 1393-1394.)

In the First Letter to the Corinthians, St. Paul reaffirms the integral place of the Eucharist in the New Covenant. Paul also gives us added insight into the relationship between the priesthood and the Lord's Supper, stating: "Every time, then, you eat this bread and drink this cup you proclaim the death of the Lord until he comes" (1 Cor 11:26). If the Lord's Supper must be carried out "until he comes," then obviously there must be a lasting priesthood to carry out the commission given to the apostles at the Last Supper, lest Jesus' command be ignored and the New Covenant be broken.[4]

That is the simple statement of a Catholic understanding of the priesthood. Fundamentalists raise several objections to what appear to Catholics as self-evident facts. For the sake of the pursuit of truth, these objections must be seriously considered.

The first and most important is one that shocks Catholics most: the Fundamentalist claim that there is no priesthood in the New Testament, except that of Jesus Christ; that all human mediation died on Calvary; that ministry in the apostolic Church was limited to pastors, deacons, or evangelists.

Jimmy Swaggart has said that "anytime a man says he is a priest, he is breaking the law of God. By doing so, he leads others into sin and error." These words are harsh, unnecessarily vicious, and unsubstantiated in fact. While the apostles did not refer to themselves as priests, we know that they did share in the ministry of the High Priest, Jesus Christ. There are three probable reasons why the term "priest" was not applied to the leaders of the early Church. First, there was a great deal of animosity expressed in the New Testament toward Jewish priests. Second, there was undoubtedly a fear of confusing the apostles and their successors with pagan priests of that time. The early Church felt a need to distance herself from both groups. The third reason, however, was the most critical: a concern that the unique high priesthood of Jesus Christ would not be clouded over (cf. Heb 8). Just as Christ's redemptive sacrifice was effected once and for all (never to be repeated), so too is Christ's priesthood unique. However, the Eucharist, which sacramentally re-presents the sacrifice of Calvary, requires priestly ministers, as already noted. Such ministers are not priests in their own right but participate in the priesthood of Jesus Christ. This point is sometimes lost on Fundamentalists, who think the Catholic notion of priesthood in some way nullifies the unique priesthood of Jesus. When the animosity toward the Jewish and pagan priesthoods waned and the fear of theological confusion subsided, the term "priest" began to be applied, quite appropriately, to those men who shared in and continued Christ's ministry on earth. (Cf. CCC nn. 1544-1553.)

The definitive act of mediation between God and man took place in Christ's redemptive sacrifice, to be sure. However, this fact does not in any way render useless or obsolete (let alone sacrilegious or blasphemous) other, subordinate forms of mediation. Paul saw this so clearly that he put it forth as a rhetorical question: "And how can they believe unless they have heard of him? And how can they hear unless there is someone to preach? And how can men preach unless they are sent?" (Rom 10:14f). Preaching is an act of mediation. This is carried a step further in the dialogue between Philip and the Ethiopian eunuch, as the latter asks how he can understand Scripture "unless someone explains it to me" (Acts 8:31). Offering authoritative interpretations of Scripture is an act of mediation. After he understood the message, the eunuch asked to be baptized, "and Philip went down into the water with the eunuch and baptized him" (Acts 8:38). Administering the sacraments is an act of mediation.

Preaching, interpretation of Scripture, and administering of sacraments are all found in the New Testament, and all place a sacred minister between an individual believer and Christ. Of course, these acts of mediation are not obstacles to union with the Lord Jesus but are facilitators. Catholics see the ministerial priesthood in just that light. The ordained priest never takes the place of Christ but leads people to Christ the eternal High Priest. (Cf. CCC nn. 1546-1547.)

Because priests are called to imitate the pattern of Christ's life as closely as possible, an ancient tradition of the Latin Rite calls for celibate priests.[5] The priest's concern for the Church is to be total, so that his individual attention and love are centered on his ministry. However, some misunderstandings about celibacy need to be clarified. First, celibacy does not depreciate marriage; its place in the priesthood emphasizes the fact that marriage and priesthood are vocations in themselves and that both deserve one's complete commitment. Second, the rationale behind priestly celibacy is not simply a pragmatic solution for greater availability or economy. Celibacy is meant to be an eschatological sign that reminds people that "we have here no lasting city" (Heb 13:14), and that our sights need to be set on that city where God is all in all (cf. 1 Cor 15:28). It seems to me that the witness of celibacy for the sake of the kingdom is much stronger today precisely because we live in such a sex-saturated society. Third, the ecclesiastical law on priestly celibacy is not of divine origin, although surely the Lord's clear preference (cf. Mt 19:29; Lk 14:26; Mk 10:29). This means that the law does admit of exceptions. For this reason, the Church has always permitted married men of the Eastern Rites to be ordained and recently granted special permission for married Anglican clergy who have joined the Roman Catholic Church to maintain their marital and family commitments and also be admitted to the priesthood.

That having been said, what are the problems that Fundamentalists have with clerical celibacy? Swaggart quotes Paul's First Letter to Timothy, which warns against men "who forbid marriage" (1 Tim 4:3) to denounce the practice of celibacy altogether, charging that it "has caused untold immorality in the Catholic Church,"[6] but offering no proof for the charge. Despite Swaggart's allegations, however, the practice of celibacy has significant foundations in Scripture.[7] (Cf. CCC n. 1579.)

In the nineteenth chapter of Matthew, Jesus' disciples ask Him if it is preferable not to marry. In response, Jesus tells His disciples that there are some men who are incapable of sexual activity, some who have made themselves deliberately so, and others who have renounced sex freely "for the sake of God's reign," adding: "Let him accept this teaching who can" (Mt 19:12). Jesus' position regarding celibacy for the kingdom is both positive and clear in this passage.

This statement is reinforced in Luke 18:28-30 as Jesus promises a plentiful return in this age and life everlasting in the next for all who have left wife and home, parents and children for the sake of the kingdom of God. Renouncing sex for the kingdom of God is surely portrayed positively in the Gospels.

Another strong scriptural witness to celibacy occurs in

St. Matthew's Gospel as Jesus speaks with the Sadducees about the resurrection. Those who hold marriage as a necessary ideal because of the supposed "evils" of celibacy should closely examine Jesus' description of the life to come: "When people rise from the dead, they neither marry nor are given in marriage but live like angels in heaven" (Mt 22:30). The life of celibacy is meant to reflect that situation, indeed to fore-shadow it by reminding people of the life to come. That is what the Church intends when she asks her priests to serve as "eschatological signs."

In addition to the Gospels, St. Paul's First Letter to the Corinthians provides some final and significant support for the practice of priestly celibacy. In Chapter 7 Paul advises men and women to marry in order to avoid immorality but states that "given my preference, I should like you to be as I am" (1 Cor 7:7). Paul makes it clear that he is celibate, later explaining why such a lifestyle is preferable to marriage: "The unmarried man is busy with the Lord's affairs, concerned with pleasing the Lord; but the married man is busy with this world's demands and occupied with pleasing his wife. This means he is divided" (1 Cor 7:32f). The obvious message of the New Testament is that a celibate clergy is to be preferred. The Catholic Church makes that preference a norm, and that tradition has served the Gospel and the Church very well throughout her twenty-century history.

A final and common criticism of the priesthood centers upon the fact that priests are addressed as "Father." Funda-mentalists condemn this practice, citing Matthew 23:9 to support their position: "Do not call anyone on earth your father. Only one is your father, the One in heaven." If we turn to the First Letter of John, however, we find that the writer of that epistle appears to have violated Jesus' injunction when he speaks to the elders of the community thus: "I address you, fathers, for you have known him who is from the beginning" (1 Jn 2:14). In point of fact, what Jesus condemned was the giving to any human the honor or adoration proper to God. That same passage speaks of calling no one teacher, either; however, thousands of physicians, professors, and Protestant ministers are called "doctor," which means "teacher." Would these critics also take this passage so literally that they would deny children the right to address their male parents as "fathers"? We must distinguish, then, between the letter of the law and the spirit of the law, as did the author of 1 John. St. Paul was very forthright on his spiritual fatherhood as he reminded his spiritual children: "Granted you have ten thousand guardians in Christ, you have only one father. It was I who begot you in Christ Jesus through my preaching of the gospel" (1 Cor 4:15).[8] The title of "Father" does not place a priest on a pedestal, creating distance between a priest and his people. On the contrary, it serves as a reminder of the depth of the relationship that exists: that because of Christ, His Gospel, and His Church, all relationships in the Church are essentially familial.

The most serious objections raised to the ministerial priesthood by Fundamentalists concern the unique priesthood of Jesus Christ and the priesthood of all believers. The Catholic Church accepts unequivocally the necessity of a ministerial priesthood and the priesthood of the faithful, "each of them in its own special way . . . a participation in the one priesthood of Christ."[9] The ordained priest shares in the priesthood of believers by virtue of Baptism, and in the priesthood of Christ in the Sacrament of Holy Orders. The ministerial priesthood and the priesthood of the faithful are united at the altar in the Eucharistic Sacrifice as they join their prayer to the eternal intercession of Jesus Christ, in total fidelity to Him Who is the Church's Lord. (Cf. CCC nn. 1546-1547.)

6

Do Catholics Worship Mary and the Other Saints?

Catholics, often insulted by this question, frequently refuse to answer it on that account. A non-response, however, is not helpful for a variety of reasons, not the least of which is that it is an extremely important question — the answer to which determines whether or not one is a Christian. (Cf. CCC nn. 1674-1676, 2132, 2141.)

The relationship between Catholics and Mary mystifies so many non-Catholic Christians, and we are equally mystified by their strange silence about her — a silence that is awkward and uncomfortable, a silence that is broken only once a year at Christmastime because ancient carols force believers to acknowledge and sing of the Virgin who became the Mother of the Messiah. Of course, not all non-Catholic Christians fall into this category: Eastern Orthodox devotion to the Mother of God is very strong; many Anglicans and Lutherans share our convictions about the Blessed Virgin, and one of the best books on the Rosary was written by a Methodist minister.[1] By and large, though, Protestants in general and Fundamentalists in particular have not followed the example of John the Beloved Disciple by making room in their homes for the Mother of Our Lord (cf. Jn 19:27).

Catholics need to become better spokespersons for Marian devotion, both in their articulation and in their understanding of its scriptural basis. In many circumstances, an honest dialogue brings to light that the problem of Fundamentalists with Mary is not so much Mary herself as the way she is presented. Such people need to be challenged forthrightly and charitably to think about Mary and to reflect on their usual silence (if not also their not-so-unusual hostility) in her regard. This presentation will seek, not to rouse Fundamentalists' sensibilities to Marian devotion, but to raise their consciousness to an appreciation of the role of Mary in her Son's work of salvation. (Cf. CCC n. 971.)

The teaching of the Church is clear: Jesus Christ is the sole Mediator between God and man. No other person in heaven or on earth can take His place. The role of Mary or any other saint is to lead the believer to Christ. This subordinate form of mediation derives its meaning and effectiveness from the Lord Himself and is not something the saints possess on their own. Where, then, does Mary fit into the picture? (Cf. CCC n. 970.)

Throughout the New Testament one finds references to Mary.[2] In fact, at every significant juncture in Our Lord's life, one finds Mary on the horizon. When God began His plan for our redemption, He sent to Nazareth an angel who hailed a woman as "highly favored," or "full of grace," to be the human partner in this divine enterprise (cf. Lk 1:28). When the Babe was born in Bethlehem, He came forth into our world not from heaven but from the womb of the Virgin Mary (cf. Mt 1:25; Lk 2:7). As the Child was presented to the Lord in the Temple of Jerusalem on the fortieth day, the old prophet Simeon singled out His Mother, Mary, for special mention as a woman destined to be the Mother of Sorrows (cf. Lk 2:35). Twelve years later, after another Temple visit, the Boy Jesus returned with His Mother and foster father to Nazareth and was subject to them (cf. Lk 2:51). It was Mary who prodded her Son into action at Cana to work His first miracle, launching Him on His public ministry (cf. Jn 2:3). And it was Mary who stood by His side at the foot of the cross and was given to John as the Mother of the Church (cf. Jn 19:26f). Finally, as the Church was waiting to be born in the Upper Room, while the disciples prayed for the Pentecost gift of the Spirit, Luke tells us that Mary was in their midst (cf. Acts 1:14). (Cf. CCC nn. 963-972.)

Three passages of Johannine origin must be considered in greater depth, two of them already noted in passing. Most serious Scripture commentators agree that John has the most highly developed theology and literary style of all the New Testament writers. The structure of John's Gospel is a masterpiece by which even the arrangement of material or the introduction of certain people advances the theological agenda of the evangelist. For example, the unnamed "beloved disciple" is generally regarded to stand as a symbol for the ideal Christian in every age who stands with Jesus to the end — and beyond. Another figure of prominence, however, is the Mother of the Lord, who appears only twice (unnamed also). Her appearances are at the beginning and the end of her Son's public ministry, as the evangelist used the Hebraic device of "inclusion" to frame the Lord's earthly career.[3]

It is interesting that John, who has no infancy narrative, does feel compelled to place Mary in the midst of events. Thus he shows her to be the one responsible for Christ's first miracle, when He responded to her firm faith, although He had already told her rather succinctly: "My hour has not yet come" (Jn 2:4). Jesus' responsiveness to His Mother in this passage has provided Christians throughout the ages with the basis for seeking Mary's intercession on their behalf.

The Lord's earthly ministry ended on Calvary, with the beloved disciple and Mary brought into a unique relationship with each other by the dying Christ. The beloved disciple, representative of every committed Christian, in that moment was given the Mother of Christ to be his own Mother. The physical maternity of Mary was thus extended and expanded to include now a spiritual motherhood of the Church, her Son's brothers and sisters. Just as she brought Christ's physical Body into the world, now she would play a role on behalf of His mystical Body (the Church). Mary did not ask for the role, nor did the Church give it to her; it was nothing less than her divine Son's dying wish for her and for His Church (cf. Jn 19:26f). (Cf. CCC n. 2679.)

The theme of the woman who is the Mother of the Church reaches a crescendo in Revelation 12. Even astute readers are brought up short as they try to unravel the symbolism. Is the woman, laboring to give birth, Mary or the Church? The author of Revelation was so skillful a writer that both interpretations are possible, and both are probably intended. Catholic theology sees the parallels as more than a happy coincidence, for the roles of Mary and the Church overlap or intersect at many points. This was apparent by the use of "inclusion" in the Gospel of John and is equally apparent in the Book of Revelation through the double symbolism employed by the sacred author.

Catholics look on Mary, above all, as a model and guide. By her "yes" to the will of the Father at the Annunciation, Mary became the first and best Christian ever to live. Her life is a testimony to the wonderful things that can happen when the human person cooperates with the divine plan. In agreeing to be the human vessel that brought the Messiah into the world, Mary played an essential part in Christ's salvific mission. She manifested Christian humility and obedience when she responded to God's will: "I am the servant of the Lord. Let it be done to me as you say" (Lk 1:38). Her faith in God and her response to His will mark Mary as the first human being to accept Christ, body and soul, as she welcomed Him into her very self. The Church ever since echoes the words of Mary's kinswoman Elizabeth, as she proclaims: "Blest is she who trusted that the Lord's words to her would be fulfilled" (Lk 1:45). (Cf. CCC n. 973.)

Catholics seek Mary's intercession just as they seek the intercession of all good Christians, living and dead — for all are alive in Christ (cf. 1 Cor 15:22). This Christian concern for one another manifested through intercessory prayer is as old as the Church.[4] If we, who still sin, can pray effectively for one another, why not the saints in glory? The favorite prayer of Christians to the Mother of Christ is the "Ave Maria," so often the inspiration for great musical compositions. The words are simple: "Hail Mary, full of grace, the Lord is with thee; blessed art thou among women, and blessed is the fruit of thy womb, Jesus. Holy Mary, Mother of God, pray for us sinners, now and at the hour of our death. Amen." (Cf. CCC n. 975.)

What could a Fundamentalist find objectionable in a prayer whose roots are so biblical? The first half is a direct quote from Lk 1:28, 42, while the second half affirms the divinity of Christ, the fallen state of man, human mortality, and the power of intercessory prayer. (Cf. CCC nn. 956, 969, 2673-2678.)

This prayer finds its way into the Rosary, which is a meditative form of prayer, combining elements of formulaic prayer and reflection on the mysteries of redemption.[5] Catholics do not see in the Rosary the "vain repetition of words" that Fundamentalists see because Catholics are not seeking to "win a hearing by the sheer multiplication of words" (Mt 6:7). On the contrary, the stress is not on the words but on the attitude and atmosphere of prayer that is created, allowing the believer to become lost in reflection on the divine and enabling God to speak rather than oneself. (Cf. CCC n. 2708.)

Some non-Catholics are taken aback by the practice of novenas, which have the appearance of the magical to the uninitiated. A novena is simply a set of prayers offered to Our Lord or His Blessed Mother or one of the other saints, over a period of nine days, weeks, or months. The number nine is not magical but takes its origins from the nine days from the Ascension to Pentecost, when the Church made the first novena as the apostles and disciples prayed for the Holy Spirit to come upon them (cf. Acts 1 and 2).

Similarly, Catholics use medals and statues not as talismans or as objects of worship in violation of the First Commandment; rather, these things are intended to be reminders or aids to devotion that focus one's attention on prayer and the practice of virtue. It would be a rare husband who did not carry in his wallet a photo of his wife and children, not because he worships the photo or his family but because he loves his family and wishes to have a visual representation of them on his person. Nor have I ever heard a Fundamentalist take offense at the presence of statues of our country's heroes at national monuments. If the heroes of the nation can be so honored, why not the heroes of the Church? Catholics use sacred art in exactly the same way, never fashioning "idols" for false worship (cf. Dt 5:8). (Cf. CCC n. 1670.)

Prayer to Mary, like all Marian devotion, is not an end in itself but is intended to be a means by which one is led to a deeper union with her Son. Classical spirituality even had a Latin maxim to illustrate the point: *Ad Jesum per Mariam* ("To Jesus through Mary"). True devotion to Mary never obscures the uniqueness of Christ because Catholics know that the only command of Mary recorded in the Scriptures is one that must be scrupulously obeyed: "Do whatever he [Jesus] tells you" (Jn 2:5).

The two principal Marian doctrines are grossly misunderstood by Fundamentalists and require careful explanation. Dogmas of faith about Mary are Christological and ecclesiological in their intent. Simply put, that means that the Church sees her reflections on Mary as saying more about Jesus and the Church than about Mary herself, who joins Jesus and the Church because of her unique position in the economy of salvation.

The doctrine of the Immaculate Conception of Mary holds that no stain of Adam's sin touched the Blessed Virgin. That says something about Mary, of course, but it points in two other directions as well. First, it says that this privilege accorded to her was in virtue of her role as Mother of the Messiah, in order to make her a worthy dwelling for Him. Second, it is a reminder that through Christ's redeeming Death and Resurrection, all believers have the stain of original sin washed from their souls in the waters of Baptism. Fundamentalists become nervous with this doctrine because they think it removes Mary from the rest of humanity and raises her to the level of a goddess. They point to the fact that in her Magnificat Mary sings of "God my Savior" (Lk 1:47), thus implicitly acknowledging her own need for redemption. Catholic theology explains this by asserting that Mary was indeed redeemed by God through "prevenient grace." This term of scholastic theology simply means that God spared Mary from sin, crediting to her in advance the benefits of her Son's redemptive sacrifice, so that she could sinlessly bear the sinless Son of God. It is important to remember that the concept of time is a human construct and that God lives in an eternal present; therefore, what sounds so strange to us is, in fact, not at all strange for Him. To deny this possibility is to limit the power of God. (Cf. CCC nn. 490-493.)

The dogma of Mary's Assumption teaches that the Mother of the Lord was taken into heaven, body and soul, since no decay should touch the body of her who bore the Messiah. Christians say they believe "in the resurrection of the body"; the doctrine of the Assumption merely asserts God's acknowledgment of Mary's worthiness to anticipate (from the earth-bound perspective of human time, again) the fullness of salvation as both Mother of Christ and Mother of the Church.[6] Once more, we see a Christological and ecclesiological dimension. The reward given to Mary is given ultimately in virtue of her divine maternity. It likewise points toward the resurrection of the dead, which is the hope of the whole Church. (Cf. CCC n. 966.)

Mary's privileges are promises. What God has done for her, He is willing to do for all the other members of His Son's Church. Mary's experience is unique only from the temporal point of view, in that the experience of salvation (her Immaculate Conception) and the experience of resurrection (her Assumption) are possible for all believers. In the most basic terms possible, the difference between Mary and the rest of the Church is that her possession of these gifts is present and real, while ours is an event of the future, for which one hopes and prays. (Cf. CCC n. 972.)

Fundamentalists' denunciations of Catholic teaching on Mary become particularly strident on the question of Mary's perpetual virginity. No Christian who takes the Scriptures seriously can doubt Mary's virginity up to the birth of Jesus, since the Gospels are so clear on this point (cf. Mt 1:18; Lk 1:34). However, the Church teaches that Mary was a virgin not only when she conceived the Lord in her womb but for the rest of her life. (Cf. CCC nn. 496-507.)

Jimmy Swaggart and other Fundamentalists contest this point, however, claiming that "anyone with even cursory knowledge of the Bible is therefore hard-pressed to accept the Catholic position that Mary remained a virgin throughout her life." He points to Matthew 1:24f, which states that Joseph did not know Mary until she bore Jesus, arguing that this is "implicit indication that Joseph did not know Mary until Mary delivered Jesus, but that he did afterward."[7] Swaggart's conclusion, however, is faulty, since the word "until" is defined by *Webster's Dictionary* as "up to the time that" but also "when or before." The word "until" implies no action afterward in either standard English or biblical usage.[8]

In addition to his erroneous conclusions based upon Matthew 1:24f, Jimmy Swaggart claims that "the Bible plainly lists the children of Joseph and Mary — conceived and born after Jesus' birth." He cites Mark 3:31-33, which refers to Jesus' "mother and his brothers," in defense of his position. Were Swaggart to move beyond a "cursory" understanding of the Bible, however, he would realize that the same word used for brothers in this passage (and others) is also rendered as "brethren" elsewhere. A deficiency in Hebrew and Aramaic makes it difficult to discern whether the word carries the connotation of blood brother, cousin, or some relation between the two in any one passage. One cannot prove that Mary had other children from the Gospel accounts for this reason. (Cf. CCC n. 500.)

But why does the Church make such an issue over Mary's perpetual virginity? First of all, because it is a matter of preserving the truth. The Church has always taught that Mary was a perpetual virgin. This information can be gleaned from many sources, but especially from the earliest liturgical prayers in which reference is made to "the Virgin." If Mary had not remained a virgin until death, why speak of her after the birth of Christ as such? If one has an uncle who is a bachelor, he is rightly referred to as one's "bachelor uncle." If he marries and thus ceases to be a bachelor, calling him a "bachelor uncle" would be senseless. In the same way, the early Church spoke of Mary as "the Virgin" precisely because of the belief that she lived and died a virgin. When this teaching was questioned in later centuries, we find the addition of the adverb "ever." Thus do the Creed of Epiphanius (c. 374), the Second Council of Constantinople (553), and the Lateran Council (649) all speak of the "ever-Virgin Mary." Augustine, Jerome, and Cyril of Alexandria followed the same usage, as did Protestant reformers Luther, Calvin, and Zwingli.

The doctrine of Mary's perpetual virginity is not a statement that sex is bad, but it is an important statement regarding Mary's single-heartedness and the uniqueness of her vocation. She was called to be the Mother of the Messiah; no other work could surpass it, and hence it was fitting that no other fruit should come forth from the womb that carried the Redeemer of humanity.[9] With no proof for other children born to Mary,[10] and the weight of twenty centuries of Tradition to the contrary, the burden rests on those who would deny Mary's perpetual virginity.

Some non-Catholic Christians express concern over Catholic involvement with visions or apparitions. Such occurrences are not easily accepted by the Church, but the Church also believes that "nothing is impossible with God" (Lk 1:37). If God could reveal Himself or send intermediaries to do the same in both the Old and New Testaments (even after the Lord's Resurrection),[11] why should this be out of the question today? Any apparitions approved by the Church (whether of Our Lord to St. Margaret Mary or of the Blessed Virgin at Lourdes or Fátima) have a remarkable similarity of theme; there is no new revelation but the restatement of the heart of the Gospel message: "Reform your lives and believe in the gospel!" (Mk 1:15).[12] This is no more and no less than the message of most Fundamentalist preachers. (Cf. CCC n. 67.)

Some Fundamentalists, citing passages like John 2:4 or Mark 3:31ff, contend that Jesus did not venerate His Mother and perhaps actually repudiated her. Nothing like that can be gathered from the Scriptures. On the contrary, as a good Jew and loyal son of the covenant, Christ took seriously the divine commandment to "honor thy father and thy mother." Hence, we learn that after His being found in the Temple, He returned to Nazareth and was obedient to Mary and Joseph (cf. Lk 2:51). Beyond that, any passage that appears in some way to diminish Mary's role is found, upon closer examination, to increase her prestige because Jesus used such occasions to downplay mere physical claims to fame and set them in the broader context of spiritual discipleship. Mary thus had a twofold right to honor: first, as Mother of the Lord; second, as one who heard God's Word and reflected on it in her heart (cf. Lk 2:19).

A great deal of time and space has been spent in discussing the place of Mary in the life of the Church. The chapter title also included "the other saints." What about them? First of all, it is good to observe that the task was to consider "Mary and the other saints." In other words, Mary is a saint. This means she was a human being like us (albeit specially chosen and honored by God). Therefore, what has been said about devotion to her or recourse to her intercession applies to the other saints as well.

The Church honors certain men and women with the title of "saint" because their holiness warrants it but also because the Church on earth can benefit from their example. Patron saints for various professions or nations are holy people who are offered to believers as models worthy of emulation. Feast days of saints are opportunities to celebrate throughout the year Christ's victory over Satan in the lives of His Chosen People. Such a devotion reminds us that God is glorious in His saints (cf. 2 Thes 1:10), and that every Christian is called to be a saint, even if never publicly honored by the Church through the process of canonization.[13] The universal call to holiness is celebrated each year on November 1, All Saints' Day, as the Church honors all the holy men and women of every time and place (most of them known only to God) who stand before the throne of the Lamb (cf. Rev 7). (Cf. CCC nn. 828, 1717, 2030, 2156.)

To answer the critical question, then, we Catholics do not worship Mary and the other saints. We accord them special honor because of their lives of faithful witness, and we seek their intercession before the Lord as all believers in heaven and on earth unite their prayers to the perfect prayer of Christ.

Mary is a sign of hope for Christians. Wordsworth put it poetically and almost biblically when he spoke of her as "our tainted nature's solitary boast." In Mary, God returned humanity to the innocence of Eden; thus she is a sign and promise of what the Lord will do for all who follow her example of fidelity.

In the Scriptures, Mary prophesied that "all ages to come shall call me blessed" (Lk 1:48). Catholics consider it a privilege to fulfill that prophecy, for one cannot ignore this woman, lest one risk distorting the Gospel itself. (Cf. CCC n. 971.)

7

Is the Mass Biblical?

ow does the believer maintain contact with the Risen Christ? Did the first apostles and disciples of Jesus have an advantage over those to follow, in terms of a relationship of intimacy with the Lord? Such questions have been matters of concern to Christians throughout the ages, and even within the New Testament itself we obtain hints of such concerns. We also see how the sacred writers attempted to answer those questions.

The sixth chapter of John's Gospel deals with such issues insightfully and effectively, but Luke does so with poetry, art, and sensitivity. He tells a story. The Emmaus pericope or key text (Lk 24:13-35) is a story of rare charm and beauty that teaches theology by means of a drama. To the plea of the disciples ("Stay with us"), the Stranger responds not with a dissertation but with a ritual, familiar action ("the breaking of the bread"). At the very moment the disciples recognize their Guest as the Risen One, He vanishes from their sight. (Cf. CCC n. 1329.)

What is St. Luke's point? This story is his answer to the two questions raised at the outset. The contemporary disciple encounters the Risen Christ in the Eucharist. And, no, those of yesteryear who walked and talked with Jesus during His earthly life and ministry have no advantage over us because we encounter the very same Christ that they did. That assertion is supported by the fact that the sacred writer shows Jesus in His glorious and risen Body disappearing the minute the disciples recognize Him in the signs and symbols of the Eucharist, for the physical Christ is a redundancy when the sacramental Christ is present.

Samuel Terrien has demonstrated very convincingly[1] that the whole of the divine-human relationship chronicled in the Scriptures is one of progressive intimacy: from the conversations between God and Adam in Eden, to the covenant with Abraham, to the giving of the Law, to the Incarnation. In fact, one can declare with full confidence that the story of God's involvement with His people is merely the fulfillment of His desire to be near to those He loves. The Eucharist is the special way that the Lord Jesus makes good on His promise to be with us until the end of time (cf. Mt 28:20). (Cf. CCC n. 1380.)

Just what is the Eucharist? Definitions are inadequate, but let us try this: The Eucharist is a sacrificial meal commemorating and offering salvation. It is the making present again of the Lord's Supper, in which Jesus realizes His destiny and commits Himself, present under the appearances of bread and wine, to His act of self-donation in fidelity and love. (Cf. CCC nn. 1322-1332.)

Jesus chose a meal to do this for many reasons. A meal is a most significant human experience. One only shares a table with friends and family; inviting someone to dinner is an expression of esteem. Jews looked on a meal as a ritual action, and the particular meal that Jesus chose (the Passover) was replete with religious meaning. By using the Passover meal, Jesus could take advantage of past Jewish history to illustrate what He was about to do; because of its religious and instructional character, He could teach His disciples the very basics of being a follower of His (cf. Jn 13—17; Lk 22:14-36). Familiarity with the twelfth chapter of Exodus is most beneficial for a proper understanding of the Christian Eucharist, for notions like blood, sacrifice, lamb, and memorial feast have their roots firmly planted in the Passover experience. (Cf. CCC nn. 1333-1340.)

Jesus spoke His word of love (Liturgy of the Word) and then gave the proof of that love by declaring His intention to suffer and die for His followers, and by presenting this meal as the promise and fulfillment of that salvific event (Liturgy of the Eucharist). (Cf. CCC nn. 1348-1355.)

Thus the Last Supper points toward Calvary, where all men of all time were saved (cf. Heb 9). If all people were saved in that one momentous occasion, why does the Church continue to offer the Sacrifice of the Mass? Because the salvation promised and earned is conditional; because it is contingent upon our acceptance of Jesus, our desire to be saved, and our living of a lifestyle that demonstrates an understanding of what life in Christ means. Since we were not present, we need to be reminded of what God has done for us. Our remembrance and ritual reenactment of the event make it happen again — for us. (Cf. CCC nn. 1341-1344, 1362-1367.)

Jesus offers His Body and Blood; His Death brings us life, just as the blood of the lamb saved the Hebrews. Washed in His Blood, we are cleansed from sin (cf. Heb 9:14) and made incredibly alive to God's designs for our salvation. Receiving the Body of Christ makes each of us as individuals to form the Body of Christ, which is His Church. In other words, the Eucharistic Body of Christ is offered to us, so that we can become more clearly the ecclesial Body of Christ. This is also why Catholics refuse to practice intercommunion with other

Christians, since this sacrament celebrates union not only with Christ but also union with the Church. To feign unity is to make of the Eucharist a sign of contradiction. (Cf. CCC nn. 1368-1372.)

How does the marvelous exchange of gifts occur — Christ for bread and wine? Jesus told us to remember Him, for memory is a most powerful human faculty. For a Jew, to remember someone or some event was to present again the benefits of that relationship. That is why, of all Christ's commandments, the one to remember Him is the most critical. If we fail to remember Jesus, if we fail to renew His sacrificial meal, we will cease to be Christians because we will no longer hear those words of love, no longer receive His Body and Blood as their proof, no longer be challenged and inspired to love our fellowman as He commanded us. Therefore, memory is key; sacred memory leads to sacred reality. (Cf. CCC nn. 1341-1344.)

Furthermore, when the Church gathers in faith to do what Jesus commanded and speaks His words, "This is my body to be given for you. . . . This cup is the new covenant in my blood which will be shed for you . . ." (Lk 22:19f), our words are no longer our own but God's. The Word of God overtakes the elements of bread and wine and transforms them into the Divine Presence. Jesus our God comes among us again. Through faith, we acknowledge Him as present and look forward to that time when He will come again in glory and no longer under veiled signs. (Cf. CCC nn. 1373-1377.)

The Jesus Who comes in this mysterious manner also remains with us under the sacred signs. For this reason, the Church has always encouraged devotion to the Blessed Sacrament. We come to the Christ of the Eucharist with our present sorrows and ask Him to unite them to His, which were nailed to the cross. For through the cross, we hope to share in His Resurrection. The Eucharistic Jesus is a consolation but also a challenge: to be all that we are meant to be, to become one family because we are fed with one Bread, to love one another as He has loved us. (Cf. CCC nn. 1378-1381.)

Ironically enough, this sacrament of unity and peace has often been a sacrament of division, in the sense that so many controversies have surrounded its interpretation. Our age is no different. (Cf. n. 1336.)

The Catholic Church ascribes a literal meaning to the words spoken by Jesus at the Last Supper, largely because of the solemn nature of the occasion and the clear meaning of the words. This was Jesus' final meal with His disciples before He was to be betrayed and crucified; undoubtedly, Jesus would not want His disciples to misunderstand His words in these His final hours. Thus Jesus did not address the apostles by means of a parable; He offered no explanation for His words, merely the words themselves: "This is my body"; "This is my blood." Even if Jesus would have offered some symbolic interpretation for His words, which He did not, bread and wine would make a poor metaphor for death. It was only by relating them to His own flesh that they acquired meaning. (Cf. CCC nn. 1337-1340.)

The tone of Jesus' words at the Last Supper also supports the belief in the Real Presence of Christ in the Eucharist. Luke's Gospel shows us the present and immediate nature of Jesus' words as He breaks the bread and says: "This is my body to be given for you" (Lk 22:19). Jesus then took the cup of wine and said: "This cup is the new covenant in my blood, which will be shed for you" (Lk 22:20). In order to seal a Semitic covenant, a real victim was required (Gen 15:7-18; Ex 24:5f), not a symbolic representation. Jesus Christ was and is that real Victim and the great High Priest, Who seals the new covenant in His Blood. And Jesus delegated a participation in His priesthood to His apostles as He commanded them to offer the Eucharist in remembrance of Him (Lk 22:19). (Cf. CCC nn. 1373-1377.)

Scriptural evidence for the belief in the Real Presence of Christ in the Eucharist is not limited to the Gospel accounts of the Last Supper. In Paul's First Letter to the Corinthians, he contrasts the Eucharist with pagan sacrifices. In Chapter 10 St. Paul asks: "Is not the cup of blessing we bless a sharing in the blood of Christ? And is not the bread we break a sharing in the body of Christ?" (1 Cor 10:16). Paul goes on to describe the mystical union achieved by the Body of Christ through the Eucharist: "Because the loaf of bread is one, we, many though we are, are one body, for we all partake of the one loaf" (1 Cor 10:17).

Chapter 11 of Paul's First Letter to the Corinthians yields further evidence to support the belief in the Real Presence. In speaking about the "Lord's Supper," Paul admonishes the Church at Corinth for their behavior: "Every time, then, you eat this bread and drink this cup, you proclaim the death of the Lord until he comes! This means that whoever eats the bread and drinks the cup of the Lord unworthily sins against the body and blood of the Lord. A man should examine himself first; only then should he eat of the bread and drink of the cup. He who eats and drinks without recognizing the body eats and drinks a judgment on himself" (1 Cor 11:26-29). Paul is clearly speaking of the Eucharist, for an account of Jesus' words and actions at the Last Supper immediately precedes this passage. Furthermore, such a strong admonition is only sensible if we are indeed dealing with, as Paul says, "the body and blood of the Lord." The severity of Paul's criticism indicates the unique nature of the Lord's Supper as a true communion with Christ, and places it well beyond the status of a "simple memorial supper."[2] (Cf. CCC n. 1385.)

Of course, most Fundamentalists question the sacrificial nature of the Eucharist, holding for only a sacred meal. The meal aspect is undoubtedly important. However, the meal takes its significance from the sacrifice. This is most obvious from all the scriptural texts that speak of the Body to be given up and the Blood to be poured out as future events. Holy Thursday's covenantal meal of promise is fulfilled in Good Friday's covenantal sacrifice (cf. 1 Cor 11:26). (Cf. CCC nn. 1362-1372.)

Perhaps even more significant than evidence for the Real Presence found in Paul's writings, however, is that found in Jesus' discourse on the bread of life in John's Gospel. In Chapter 6, Jesus informed a large crowd of people who had followed Him that they should not be "working for perishable food but for food that remains unto life eternal" (Jn 6:27). Jesus had just performed the miracle of the multiplication of the loaves and fishes and then encouraged the crowd to seek eternal food, a food that the Son of Man will give them. The crowd questioned Jesus further and asked for a sign, reminding Him that Moses had given their ancestors manna from heaven. Jesus answered that it is His Father, not Moses, Who sends true heavenly bread. When the crowd asked for this bread, Jesus proclaimed: "I myself am the bread of life. No one who comes to me shall ever be hungry, no one who believes in me shall ever thirst" (Jn 6:35). Jesus' words are at least partially metaphorical, drawing a distinction between physical and spiritual sustenance, but not wholly so. When Jesus concluded this segment of His discourse, the crowd began to murmur in protest. Jesus claimed to be the bread that came down from heaven, but the crowd asked: "Is this not Jesus, the son of Joseph? Do we not know his father and mother? How can he claim to have come down from heaven?" (Jn 6:41f). Clearly, the crowd questioned Jesus' words on a literal level, as do most Fundamentalists. (Cf. CCC n. 1336.)

In response to these questions, Jesus again addressed the crowd. Jesus reaffirmed His message to the crowd: "I myself am the living bread come down from heaven. If anyone eats this bread he shall live forever; the bread I will give is my flesh for the life of the world" (Jn 6:51). Once again, the crowd questioned Jesus: "How can he give us his flesh to eat?" (Jn 6:52). Jesus' reply was authoritative and direct: "Let me solemnly assure you, if you do not eat the flesh of the Son of Man and drink his blood, you have no life in you. He who feeds on my flesh and drinks my blood has eternal life, and I will raise him up on the last day. For my flesh is real food and my blood real drink. The man who feeds on my flesh and drinks my blood remains in me, and I in him" (Jn 6:53-56). The Greek word used by John in this passage for "feeds" is not the regular verb "to eat," but a very realistic verb that translates roughly as "to munch or gnaw." Clearly, Jesus' discourse cannot be limited to a purely symbolic level.

If there is any doubt that Jesus intended the bread-of-life discourse to carry literal connotations, the final reaction of the crowd should dispel it: "After hearing his words, many of the disciples remarked, 'This sort of talk is hard to endure! How can anyone take it seriously?' " (Jn 6:60). The writer of the Gospel goes on to note that as a result of Jesus' words, "many of his disciples broke away and would not remain in his company any longer" (Jn 6:66). In the face of this reaction, Jesus neither gave a symbolic interpretation to His words nor informed the disciples that they misunderstood Him; rather, He merely asked the Twelve if they also wished to leave Him (cf. Jn 6:67). Peter gave the group's response to His question, and his should be ours: "Lord, to whom shall we go? You have the words of eternal life" (Jn 6:68). Some Fundamentalists retort that Jesus also used other metaphors to describe Himself, as in saying, "I am the gate" (Jn 10:9). While that is certainly true, it is equally true that no one reacted negatively to such a metaphor, and no one left His company because of it. Thus one can see that we are looking at a very different situation here, one requiring a literal interpretation — if all the facts of the Johannine account are to make sense.

In spite of the scriptural evidence to the contrary, some claim that the doctrine of the Real Presence of Christ in the Eucharist is contrary to Scripture. We learn from St. Paul's Letter to the Romans, they contend, that Christ endured death only once: "We know that Christ being raised from the dead will never die again; death no longer has dominion over him" (Rom 6:9). Clearly, Christ died but once for our sins. The celebration of the Eucharist, however, neither merely recalls nor actually repeats the sacrifice of the cross, but renders it sacramentally present. As Yahweh gave life to the people of Israel by giving them manna from heaven (Ex 16:4), so too does His Son, Jesus Christ, communicate His eternal life by giving His followers the bread of life, which is His flesh and blood. Catholics do not believe that Christ dies over and over again in each Mass but that through the Mass the benefits of the Lord's Death and Resurrection are offered to believers today. (Cf. CCC nn. 1366-1367.)

Information about the Eucharistic beliefs of the early Church can also be found in secular sources. In his *Annals*, the first-century Roman historian Tacitus makes mention of the Christian religion. He states that the Death of Christ at the hands of Pontius Pilate "checked the abominable superstition for the while," noting that belief in Christ broke out again in Rome itself, "the great reservoir and collecting ground of every kind of filth and depravity."[3] As historian Donald Dudley notes, "the depravity and filth specifically associated with early Christianity were charges of cannibalism, infanticide, and incest brought against it by a misunderstanding of the nature of the Eucharist."[4] Both Tertullian and Minucius Felix corroborate Dudley's assertion, since both give considerable attention in their second-century writings to the charge of cannibalism being leveled against the Church. A belief in the Real Presence thus clearly existed in the early Church, for no "simple memorial supper" would have evoked such specific and violent charges from the general pagan populace.

In his letter to his "Catholic friends," Jimmy Swaggart states: "We know that the form of the Mass developed slowly over the years."[5] While it is historically accurate and quite obvious that the form of the Mass developed slowly over time, Mr. Swaggart's leap of logic in asserting that the development of the Mass precludes its having been derived from Christ and the apostles is clearly unfounded. Although the form of the Mass developed over time, its central component, the celebration of the Eucharist, was instituted by Christ Himself and handed down by the apostles. There is both scriptural and historical evidence attesting to this fact. (Cf. CCC n. 1345.)

With regard to the celebration of the Eucharist during the Mass, Jimmy Swaggart contends that "there is nothing anywhere in the Bible that even suggests such a procedure."[6] A close examination of Scripture and Church history, however, reveals distinct evidence that supports Catholic teaching on the Eucharist. The Acts of the Apostles recounts the Sunday gathering of the faithful to celebrate the Eucharist (cf. 2:42). As time went on, the synagogue Scripture service was tacked onto the Eucharist, leaving us with the Mass as we know it: a service in two parts — Liturgy of the Word and Liturgy of the Eucharist. (Cf. CCC nn. 1346-1347.)

Some critics would concede that the general outline of the Mass has a scriptural foundation but contend that the use of vestments, candles, incense, and other external aids to devotion are problematic. All of these Catholic liturgical practices have their roots in the liturgy of the Temple at Jerusalem, and we know, beyond the shadow of a doubt, that Jesus devoutly and regularly participated in the Temple liturgy. If Christ is the new High Priest and His sacrifice on Calvary has fulfilled the sacrifices of the old Law (cf. Heb 9:11ff), it is entirely appropriate to use Temple symbolism. (Cf. CCC nn. 1145-1162.)

At the Last Supper (the first Mass), Jesus prayed to His heavenly Father for the unity of all believers in Him (cf. Jn 17:20-26). The Eucharist is the sign of that unity between the individual believer and Christ, and among all the believers themselves. For this reason, Catholics celebrate the Eucharist with devotion and love until the Lord's Second Coming (cf. 1 Cor 11:26). Like the disciples on the road to Emmaus, we Catholics invite the Unknown Guest to stay with us. And like them, we are led to recognize Christ as risen and dwelling among us "in the breaking of the bread." Thus do we discover that neither Peter nor Mary Magdalene was any better off than we are, for like the Blessed Virgin herself, we bear Christ within our very selves — through the gift of the Eucharist. Catholics also wish that all Christians could know the beauty and meaning of that experience.

8

Can Priests Forgive Sins?

The first word uttered by the Risen Christ on Easter night conveyed His special Easter gift to His Church: "Peace!" It is significant that immediately following on the heels of that greeting is the Lord's commission to His apostles to forgive sins in His name: "If you forgive men's sins, they are forgiven; if you hold them bound, they are held bound" (Jn 20:23). What is the connection between the two statements?

Shalom, the Hebrew word Jesus would have used that first Easter, carries within itself so many meanings that it cannot be adequately translated by a single word. *Shalom* connotes wholeness, harmony, unity, peace, and right relationships. It harks back to the Genesis accounts that depict God and man in an intimate union of friendship and love. That union was destroyed, however, by the sin of our first parents. From that day on, sin has always obstructed the movement of the human person toward God. For peace to be found, the roadblock of sin must be removed. Hence, the link between the Resurrection gift of peace and the Resurrection gift of forgiveness.

That link is maintained by the Church in the Sacrament of Penance. Not without reason did many of the Fathers of the Church refer to Penance as "the second Baptism." They saw in this sacrament the consoling possibility of returning to baptismal innocence, the ability to have a second chance if one is only willing to repent and begin again. (Cf. CCC nn. 1446-1447.)

It has become popular nowadays to speak about whether or not a person is "saved." In truth, however, salvation is an ongoing process in a person's life in which he or she attempts to grow ever closer to God. It is with the goals of growth and reconciliation in mind that the Church provides the Sacrament of Penance for her members. As defined by the Council of Trent, the Sacrament of Penance was instituted by Christ for the purpose of reconciling the faithful to God as often as they fall into sin after Baptism.

According to the Church, there are three distinct facets of the sacrament. First and foremost is the need for contrition on the part of the sinner; that is, that he or she feel sorrow for having sinned. Forgiveness is contingent upon a desire to be forgiven, and a resolve to avoid that sin in the future. This sacrament is intended to be a true encounter between the sinful self and the forgiving Christ. Anything less is a hypocritical charade. Nothing less than a true desire to turn from sin, to change one's life, to go through a conversion experience is required. Frequently, non-Catholics have the impression that the Catholic approach to sin is one of: "Oh, well, I'll just go to confession on Saturday." Such an attitude makes a mockery of divine justice and is a parody of the Church's sacramental theology. (Cf. CCC nn. 1451-1454.)

Secondly, the sinner must confess his sins and admit to having fallen in the eyes of God. We are told in the Epistle of James to "declare [our] sins to one another" (Jas 5:16). In admitting that we have sinned, we also acknowledge our need for the healing power of Jesus Christ in our lives. (Cf. CCC nn. 1455-1458.)

The final component of the Sacrament of Penance is satisfaction. In addition to seeking the removal of the guilt of sin, the penitent should attempt to make some type of reparation for the wrongs committed. (Cf. CCC nn. 1459-1460.)

The Sacrament of Penance, while criticized by many outside the Church as unbiblical, has definite scriptural foundations. At root, it is grounded in Christ's power to forgive sins.

In the ninth chapter of St. Matthew's Gospel, the evangelist relates the story of Jesus' cure of a paralytic at Capernaum. Jesus informs the paralytic that his sins are forgiven, causing the scribes present to think that Jesus has blasphemed, for only God can forgive sins. They did not, of course, recognize Jesus as God. Jesus responds to their mental musings by ordering the paralytic: "Stand up! Roll up your mat and go home" (Mt 9:6). Jesus tells us that He issues this command in order "to help [them] realize that the Son of Man has authority on earth to forgive sins" (Mt 9:6). Jesus obviously possesses the divine authority to forgive sins. (Cf. CCC nn. 1441-1445.)

The Catholic Church maintains, on the basis of scriptural and historical data, that Christ passed on His authority to forgive sins to His disciples, for it is obvious from the Gospels that Jesus did indeed confer power and authority upon His apostles. Luke states that "Jesus now called the twelve together and gave them power and authority to overcome all demons and to cure diseases" (Lk 9:1). Clearly, the delegation of divine prerogatives to the disciples was not without precedent.

In disputing the authority of the Church to forgive sins, evangelist Jimmy Swaggart states that Peter "never suggested he could forgive sins on his own authority (as do Roman Catholic priests today)."[1] This criticism must be addressed before discussing the concrete scriptural evidence supporting the Sacrament of Penance.

When one is assessing criticism of the Church, it is often difficult to determine where honest misunderstanding ends and intellectual dishonesty begins. There is nothing wrong with a healthy discussion of doctrinal differences among Christian people, so long as it is carried out in a spirit of openness, kindness, and — most importantly — truth. Jimmy Swaggart's statement regarding Catholic priests is patently false. Swaggart continues his attack, stating that "the Roman Catholic priests say, 'Te Absolvo,' which means 'I forgive you.' "[2] While his quotation is technically correct, it is only a half-truth. Were Swaggart to offer the full quotation,[3] we would see that priests forgive sins in the name of Jesus Christ. Catholic priests have never, in the past or present, claimed to forgive sins on their own authority, as Swaggart charges. They act as representatives of Christ and forgive sins in His name, just as the apostles were given the authority to overcome demons in His name. (Cf. CCC n. 1449.)

Having explained the principle of delegated authority, we can now examine more closely the scriptural foundations of the Sacrament of Penance. Some non-Catholics question the role of the Church and her priesthood in the forgiveness of sins. Jimmy Swaggart asserts that "when they [the Catholic Church] teach people that they are to confess their sins to an unmarried priest and to expect divine forgiveness, . . . they are teaching heresy, error, and total contradiction of the Word of God."[4] Swaggart's judgmental criticism, however, can be refuted easily from the New Testament itself. Just as Jesus conferred upon His disciples the power and authority to overcome demons and to cure diseases, so too did He grant them the power and authority to forgive sins. In Matthew 18:18, Jesus says to His disciples, "I assure you, whatever you declare bound on earth shall be held bound in heaven, and whatever you declare loosed on earth shall be loosed in heaven." The power to bind and loose, in rabbinic terms, constitutes the authority to declare what is allowed and forbidden under the law. It also possesses the alternate meaning of imparting the authority to excommunicate persons from the community or to include them in it. We see St. Paul exercising this type of authority in his First Letter to the Corinthians when he bans an incestuous man from the community: "Though absent in body I am present in spirit, and have already passed sentence in the name of Our Lord Jesus Christ on the man who did this deed. United in spirit with you and empowered by Our Lord Jesus, I hand him over to Satan for the destruction of his flesh, so that his spirit may be saved on the day of the Lord" (1 Cor 5:3-5). (Cf. CCC n. 1444.)

While scriptural references to binding and loosing may not conclusively demonstrate that the apostles were given the power to forgive sins, John's Gospel leaves little doubt regarding Christ's intentions in this regard. In John 20:21, as already noted, the Risen Christ says to the apostles: "As the Father has sent me, so I send you." There is obviously a specific and deliberate delegation taking place, particularly since Christ equates His commission to the apostles with that which He Himself received from His Father. It is at this point that Christ grants the apostles definitive power and authority to forgive sins as He says to them, "Receive the Holy Spirit. If you forgive men's sins, they are forgiven them; if you hold them bound, they are held bound" (Jn 20:23). This is not a parable or analogy but a direct delegation of power and authority from Christ to His apostles. And as Christ chose followers to carry on His ministry, so too did the apostles choose successors to carry on their work (2 Tim 1:6, 2:2). (Cf. CCC n. 1461.)

Jimmy Swaggart also denies the Church's authority to forgive sins on the basis that "the confessional does not come down from New Testament times. . . . The fact is," says Swaggart, "that in the first centuries after Christ, the confessional as now used was unknown. There is no reference to it in the Bible."[5]

While Swaggart's statement regarding the confessional itself is correct, his deduction regarding the relationship between the confessional and the Church's authority to forgive sins is unfounded. Swaggart's thinking exhibits a decided inability to allow for any type of development in the Church over time, as well as the tendency to confuse the Church's Christ-granted authority to forgive sins with the external practice of the sacrament. While there is no "confessional" described in the Bible, we do find evidence that Christ conferred the authority and power for the forgiveness of sins upon his apostles, as already demonstrated. If we follow Swaggart's simplistic logic, no one who does not wear a first-century tunic should be allowed to preach the Gospel, since, as we know, neither suits and ties nor modern clerical dress were worn in New Testament times. While this example is intentionally absurd, it is analogous to Mr. Swaggart's "no confessional — no sacrament" mentality.

That said, it might be well to review the history of the Sacrament of Penance. For a long period of time, this sacrament could be received only once in a lifetime, so that most people postponed its reception until they thought death was near. Eventually the Church increased the number of times this sacrament could be received to the point of our present observance, under which it is available whenever needed. (Cf. CCC n. 1447.)

Another interesting historical note is that in the early Church, all penance given for sins was "public penance," which meant that the entire Christian community was aware of the sinfulness of one of its members. Sinners were admitted to the "order of penitents" by the local bishop to perform penances involving corporal mortification and even denial of admission to the Eucharist for months or sometimes years.

In due time, the discipline of the sacrament was again relaxed as the Church entered a new era in the development of Penance. Public penance was abolished, and a penitent could confess his sins to any priest who had received the authority of his bishop to forgive sins in the name of Christ's Church. This practice became known as "private," or "auricular," confession.

The privacy gained under this system was most welcome, but an important insight became obscured: that every sin (no matter how personal) diminishes the other members of the Body of Christ, the Church. However, the advantages of this procedure far outweigh the disadvantages, because the entire approach can be individualized to correspond to the penitent's needs, along with the guarantee of complete confidentiality. (Cf. CCC n. 1467.)

Is there a way to combine the best of the ancient tradition and the benefits of the later developments? In our own day there have been attempts to do just that. The new rite provides for the option of communal celebrations of this sacrament, which help to recapture more vividly the communal sense of sin, repentance, and reconciliation. In such services all hear the Word of God proclaimed, acknowledge their sinfulness, confess their sins privately to the priest, and then receive the saving forgiveness of Almighty God.

The emotions of true penitents should be genuine sorrow and repentance, for they have sinned against God and one another, but they should also experience sentiments of hope because the Lord has given them the means to return to Him. As God's People and Christ's Church, with confidence and trust in a merciful Father, repentant sinners approach the Sacrament of Penance and see in it a sacrament of pardon, consolation, and joy.

In spite of all the scriptural data and the positive values so immediately apparent, one must admit that the perennial stumbling block for so many non-Catholic Christians is: "Why confess to a priest?" Closer analysis reveals that the real issue at stake is probably not so much the Sacrament of Penance as the Sacrament of Holy Orders. Divine forgiveness is not being questioned as much as the necessity of a ministerial priesthood. Therefore, one final attempt to address this matter from still another angle might be useful.

In the Judeo-Christian Tradition, forgiveness has always been mediated. On Yom Kippur, the Jewish high priest spoke words of sorrow to the Lord on behalf of the people and then symbolically placed the year's sins on the head of a goat, driving him out of the community into the desert. Jesus consistently presented Himself as an agent of divine forgiveness, so much so that some charged Him with blasphemy (cf. Lk 5:21). This mediatory role, however, did not end with Christ; He clearly intended His apostles to stand in His stead vis-à-vis the Church and the world (cf. Jn 20:23; Lk 9:1; Mt 16:19). (Cf. CCC n. 771.)

Christians are not rugged individualists; they come before the throne of mercy in the company of all the redeemed. Our relationship with God is personal, of course, but it is also communal. From the Catholic perspective, the personal relationship is enhanced by the communal and not diminished by it. The presence of a priest, as the ordained representative of Christ and the Church, is a concrete sign of both the communal and individual dimensions of a Christian's salvation. His presence is also a reminder that our sins offend not only the Lord but also His mystical Body, the Church.

At the level of human psychology, one can easily see the value of confession to another person. Every human being needs to "unload," to come to grips with personal guilt, and to receive guidance and encouragement. Most importantly, all people need to hear that they are indeed forgiven and to have that forgiveness celebrated in concrete, sacramental form. Surely this realization is why other Christian bodies (e.g., Episcopalians and Lutherans) have taken a second look at the Sacrament of Penance and decided to reintroduce this rite of reconciliation into their official sacramental systems.

Christ's institution of the Sacrament of Penance, far from being unbiblical, is in accordance with God's plan for our salvation. We know that faith consists of far more than just believing in the existence of God. Faith requires that we act upon and live our belief by keeping God's laws and seeking to grow ever closer to Him. Being saved is not a stagnant, once-in-a-lifetime experience, but an ongoing response to the love and will of God. Despite our best efforts, however, we all fall short of this ideal and fall into sin. By giving us the Sacrament of Penance, Christ allows us to reconcile ourselves to Him continually and to grow steadily in our faith. The Church and her priests, in the name of Jesus Christ, carry out their divine commission by calling all members of the Body of Christ to repentance, reconciliation, and a more perfect union with their Savior, Jesus Christ. (Cf. CCC nn. 1427-1433.)

If Jesus inaugurated His Resurrection appearances to His apostles with the greeting of "Peace," we also know that He began His public ministry with the invitation, or better, the command "Repent" (Mk 1:15). The Sacrament of Penance is the means by which Catholics go through the process of repentance, so as to experience Christ's peace. Or, as the confessor assures the penitent: "The Lord has freed you from your sins. Go in peace."

9

Where Do
We Go
From Here?

Fundamentalists are especially critical of Catholic teaching about the afterlife, particularly the idea of prayers to and for the dead and "the wicked doctrine of purgatory."[1] Such criticism of Church teaching on these subjects, however, reveals a lack of understanding about what the Church actually teaches on these matters. A close examination of Scripture and Church teaching on the afterlife will illustrate many of the misconceptions underlying this criticism.

Catholic teaching on the afterlife stems from the Church's belief in the Communion of Saints and the resurrection of the dead. These doctrines hold, quite simply, that those who die in Christ do not cease to be active participants in the Body of Christ. (Cf. CCC nn. 946-948, 958.)

We know from the epistles of St. Paul that there is an essential unity within the Body of Christ. In his First Letter to the Corinthians, Paul states: "For just as the body is one and has many members, and all the members of the body, though many, are one body, so it is with Christ" (1 Cor 12:12). The Church teaches that this unity is not destroyed by death because the power of death has been overcome by the Head of the Body, Jesus Christ.

The oneness of the Body of Christ is highlighted by the fact that the entire Body experiences what has been experienced by Christ, its Head. As St. Paul tells us, "Since one died for all, all died" (2 Cor 5:14). The followers of Christ share in His Death and Resurrection, His suffering and glory, both now and for all eternity.

In St. Paul's Letter to the Romans, we are told to "look on the needs of the saints as [our] own" (Rom 12:13). This exhortation is in keeping with Paul's description of the body of believers in his First Letter to the Corinthians: "God has so constructed the body . . . that all members may be concerned for one another" (1 Cor 12:24f). Does this concern end with death? Not if the Body of Christ is a united and living entity, as Scripture tells us.

Throughout a Christian's life he should be in a state of constant prayer. Prayer may take on many forms: a prayer of praise and thanksgiving for God's goodness; a prayer of supplication for oneself or for the needs of another; an awareness of the presence of God in creation. It is not the least bit unusual to petition God on behalf of others or to ask them to pray to God on our behalf. We do so nearly every day, as did the apostles and the members of the early Church. As Paul informs the Church at Corinth: "Because of your praiseworthy service they are glorifying God for your obedient faith in the Gospel of Christ, and for your generosity in sharing with them and with all. They pray for you longingly because of the surpassing grace God has given you" (2 Cor 9:13f). The Church teaches that this concern, prayer, and unity among the members of the Body of Christ does not disintegrate with death but continues among all members of the Body, whether they be in heaven or on earth.

In his letter to his "Catholic friends," Jimmy Swaggart denies that membership in the Body of Christ survives death by denouncing the practice of praying to and for the dead: "Of course, there is no hint in the Bible of anyone ever praying to the dead — not even the apostles or disciples. The Bible says in Psalm 6:5, 'For in death there is no remembrance. . . .' "[2] Swaggart's selective quoting of Scripture to support his position, however, is problematic. If we examine a greater portion of Psalm 6, we find some important information: "Return, O Lord, save my life; For among the dead no one remembers you; in the nether world who gives you thanks?" (Ps 6:5f). The Psalmist's words imply no belief in the resurrection, which was the prevalent opinion on the afterlife throughout most of Judaism, almost until the time of Christ. The Hebrew notion of the nether world, Sheol, supposed no activity or emotion among the dead, who were thought of as surrounded by the darkness of oblivion. Swaggart's reliance upon Psalm 6 to denounce prayers to and for the dead is clearly untenable, unless he also wishes to use it completely and deny the resurrection of the dead.

The Gospel of St. Matthew gives further evidence of the feeble nature of Swaggart's criticism. In Chapter 22, the Sadducees pose a question to Jesus concerning the death of a man who had no children, and of his seven brothers all marrying his widow, and all leaving her childless. They wish Jesus to tell them whose wife this woman will be at the resurrection. The author of the Gospel, however, tells us that the Sadducees "hold there is no resurrection" (Mt 22:23), evident in the question they pose to Jesus. It was commonly thought at the time that a man could live on through his children, hence the Sadducees' emphasis on a man's brothers attempting to provide his widow with a child.

The critical part of this passage, however, is found in Jesus' reply: "You are badly misled because you fail to understand the Scriptures and the power of God" (Mt 22:29). Jesus explains that people neither marry nor are given in marriage when they rise from the dead, and He goes on to address the Sadducees' denial of the resurrection, saying: "Have you not read what God said to you, 'I am the God of Abraham, the God of Isaac, the God of Jacob'? He is the God of the living, not of the dead" (Mt 22:32). Jesus, reflecting the theology of the Pharisees, refutes the Sadducees with Scripture and gives us an indication that the oneness of the body of believers does indeed survive death, for three fathers of the Jewish faith, while dead in human terms, are yet living in their God, Who is a God of the living. (Cf. CCC nn. 366, 575.)

The idea that persons continue to live in God after death is also alluded to in the Gospel of Luke. In Chapter 16, the evangelist recounts Jesus' story of the rich man and Lazarus. After a life of suffering, Lazarus dies and is "carried to the bosom of Abraham" (Lk 16:22). The rich man, upon his death, goes to a place of torment. Jesus relates a conversation between Abraham in heaven and the rich man from the abode of the dead where he is in torment.[3] Although the final judgment at the end of time has not yet occurred, both of these men are depicted as conscious and aware, though no longer living on the earth. Clearly, Jesus would not relate such a story if God were not indeed the God of the living. Hence, a Christian's ability to pray for other members of the Body of Christ should not end with death.

In conjunction with his criticism of prayers to and for those who have died in Christ, Jimmy Swaggart also questions other Church teachings on the afterlife. He claims that there are "no indulgences to buy the sinner out of purgatory." The granting of indulgences, however, is an ancient practice in the Church and based upon the principle of the Communion of Saints and an understanding of the nature of the Body of Christ. (Cf. CCC nn. 1471-1478.)

We know from the writings of St. Paul that the Body of Christ shares a unity of fate, in a spiritual sense. As Paul says: "If one member suffers, all the members suffer with it; if one member is honored, all the members share its joy" (1 Cor 12:26). However, Paul also implies that persons may sacrifice or suffer for the good of others in the Church: "Even now I find my joy in the sufferings I endure for you. In my own flesh I fill up what is lacking in the sufferings of Christ for the sake of his body, the Church" (Col 1:24). It is this idea that undergirds the principle of indulgences. The Church may grant remission of the debt of temporal punishment for sins that have been forgiven, coming from her Lord's desire that the Church be His agent of reconciliation (cf. Jn 20:23; Mt 16:19).

Remission of this punishment is granted from the treasury of merit that has been accumulated by the sacrifices of Christ, Mary, and the other saints throughout the history of the Church.[4] This is not a payment for sins in any way, but a remission of God's just punishments because of the graces obtained for the Body, the Church, through the sacrifices and merits of the saints. One gains an indulgence by performing some work of mercy or devotion to "make up" to God for wrongs done, to show a change of heart.[5] While the guilt of sin is indeed forgiven through the Sacrament of Penance, all temporal punishment due to sin is not necessarily removed. The demands of divine justice must be met through sacrifices and prayer in this life or else be atoned for in the next.

The Judeo-Christian Tradition worships a God of justice and mercy, in Whom these attitudes are in perfect equilibrium: God's justice is His mercy; His mercy is His justice. With that balance between God's justice and mercy in mind, we move to perhaps the most misunderstood of all Catholic teachings, the doctrine of purgatory.

113

Jimmy Swaggart defines purgatory as "that doctrine that gives people a second chance after death."[6] Swaggart's conception of purgatory, however, does not square with official Catholic teaching. The *New Catholic Encyclopedia* defines purgatory as "the state, place, or condition in the next world, which will continue until the Last Judgment, where the souls of those who die in the state of grace, but not yet free from all imperfection, make expiation for unforgiven venial sins and mortal sins that have already been forgiven and, by doing so, are purified before they enter heaven." Clearly, purgatory is not a "second chance" but a state or place of purification for souls before they enter into the presence of God in heaven. The Church has based this practice, in part, upon references to expiatory sacrifices for the dead found in the Second Book of Maccabees (12:39). This book was deleted from the Old Testament by the Protestant Reformers because it contradicted their position on both purgatory and prayers for the dead. (Cf. CCC nn. 1030-1032.)

Beyond the scriptural data, however, one finds an impressive array of practices that demonstrates how basic and fundamental is a belief in purgatory and prayers for the dead. In the account of the passion of the North African martyrs Perpetua and Felicity in the year 203, one reads of how one of the martyrs saw in a dream or vision her dead brother in torment, causing her to pray for his deliverance. The result of her prayer was that she saw him again — cleansed now — and "realized he had been released from his punishment." In 211, Tertullian advised Christians to pray for their beloved dead on the anniversaries of their passing from this world. St. Augustine, in his famous *Confessions,* records this remark of his dying mother, Monica, in 387: "All I ask you is this, that wherever you may be you will remember me at the altar of the Lord."

Catacomb inscriptions dating from the very origins of Christianity reveal similar themes; for example, in one burial ground, the following can be found: "Sweet Faustina, may you live in God." "Peter and Paul, pray for Victor!" "Peter and Paul, remember Sozomen and whoever reads this."[7]

This evidently indicates that what we are considering is not a medieval accretion but something that is at the very heart of Christianity: the need to pray for the dead. Prayer for the dead, in turn, presupposes that they need to be helped and can be helped. Since both heaven and hell are eternal states, the only option is an intermediate state from which release is possible; Catholic theology calls this state "purgatory." (Cf. CCC n. 991.)

Yet another historical fact is rather convincing. We know that Jesus was a devout Jew Who attended the synagogue and went up to the Temple at Jerusalem for all the prescribed feasts. At the time of Christ (and to the present in Orthodox Judaism), prayers for the dead were offered. Three times a year (during the feasts of Booths, Passover, and Weeks) special remembrances for the dead were made. Jews still utter the "Mourner's Kaddish" after the death of a loved one for eleven months — the time Jewish Tradition assigns to the period of purification after death.[8] Since this formed an essential part of Temple worship at the time of Our Lord and since we nowhere read of His contradicting this practice, one must assume that Jesus accepted it.

Common sense and human experience demonstrate that most people (even most Christians) are not good enough at death for the experience of eternal bliss, nor bad enough for the fires of hell. Purgatory corresponds to this intuition and confirms our belief in a merciful Father Who wants all His children to be saved. Far from causing laxity or presumption, this realization should inspire the mature believer to sentiments of true gratitude and the willingness to lead a yet holier life. (Cf. CCC nn. 1030-1032.)

The doctrines of the Communion of Saints and the resurrection of the dead are among the most consoling, for they tell us we are not alone in our struggle here on earth, in our time of purification, or in our hour of glory. These teachings urge us on to a sense of Christian solidarity as the members of the Church in time and eternity find that they are not separated from one another by the chasm of death but in truth are united to one another by a bridge of prayers.

Epilogue

Dear Bob and Laurie,

Thanks for a delightful dinner at your home the other evening. I hope this Epilogue, which you requested I add to my book, will serve as a lasting thank-you for all that you and your family have meant to me.

Frankly, I was surprised at how interested you were in my work on Fundamentalism. Although you are both exemplary Catholics, I never thought heavy theological discussions really concerned you. I suspected you were mainly involved with leading good Christian lives and helping your children to do the same, with no time or inclination to go beyond such matters — which would be fine with me. Would that more Catholic couples did as much! Nevertheless, you indicated you had a personal stake in this issue because so many of your Catholic friends had been attracted to Fundamentalism or were presently flirting with it. Hence your suggestion that I write an open letter to just such people, reflecting on my experiences with fallen-away Catholics. St. Paul agonized over his fellow Jews who refused to accept Jesus as their Messiah. In a similar way, I think I can adapt his words to our present concern: "Brothers, my heart's desire, my prayer to God for the Israelites, is that they may be saved. Indeed, I can testify that they are zealous for God though their zeal is unenlightened" (Rom 10:1f). Even beyond that: "I speak the truth in Christ: I do not lie. My conscience bears me witness in the Holy Spirit that there is great grief and constant pain in my heart. Indeed, I could even wish to be separated from Christ for the sake of my brothers, my kinsmen" (Rom 9:1-3). So here goes.

I have met many fallen-away Catholics over the years. On planes, trains, and city streets, they have approached me to discuss their reasons for having left the Church. In preparation for this book, I watched Jimmy Swaggart's nightly telecast as often as possible. I also met with two former Catholics for extended conversations. The one is a family man who has become a Fundamentalist minister; the other is a wife and mother whose decision to leave the Church has divided the family down the center in regard to religious allegiance and observance. As diverse as all these people could conceivably be, they all share several common characteristics.

First, and most important, they are all sincere men and women who deeply love Our Lord. This quality alone is sufficient reason to hope and to reach out to these people.

Second, they have a strange kind of love-hate relationship with the Church. Much anger comes to the surface as they discuss their former lives in the Church. At the same time, it becomes obvious that they do indeed miss something of Catholic life and practice. Why else initiate a conversation with a priest who is a total stranger while waiting for a train to arrive? Some will also admit that when they first left the Church, they "had" to be extremely negative in order to justify in their own minds and hearts their act of separation. With the passage of time, more calm and rational evaluations have become possible.

Third, many former Catholics indicate that their emotional needs were not met in Catholicism. This criticism became more common after some renderings of the revised liturgy brought about a loss of the sense of the sacred. With much of the mystique gone from official Catholic worship and the decline in more personal devotions like novenas and Benediction, some people began to look for religious experiences that were more emotionally satisfying.

Fourth, the vast majority of lapsed Catholics I have encountered have been scandalized by the presence of sinful members in Christ's Church, especially among the clergy and Religious. What they are really saying is that they are scandalized by the humanity of the Church, forgetting that the Church — like her Lord — exists primarily for sinners: "I have come to call, not the self-righteous, but sinners" (Mt 9:13). Furthermore, they should recall that ordination to the priesthood or profession of vows does not withdraw a believer from the common lot of humanity. They also need to remember Christ's admonition to the people of His own day to obey the scribes because they were the rightful teachers, without following their example, however (cf. Mt 23:1-3).

Fifth, many converts to Fundamentalism suggest that they left the Church in the wake of postconciliar confusion in the United States, seeking religious certitude and absolutes of moral behavior. While there is good reason to sympathize with such people, it is only fair to note that the official teaching of the Church never changed and has always been clearly enunciated at the highest levels. Individual dissident theologians do not form Catholic doctrine, and all Catholics know that — or should know that.

Finally, many fallen-away Catholics apparently received very poor catechetical formation (the majority of them are, in my experience, not Catholic school graduates). So often they seem not to have heard some very basic facts of Catholic life and spirituality. One man said he had never been taught about the love and mercy of Jesus. I asked him what he thought the Sacrament of Penance or devotion to the Sacred Heart of Jesus involved; he responded with a quizzical look on his face. A woman told me the Church had kept the Bible away from her. When I asked her what she considered the first half of the Mass to be, she replied, "But they never gave me my own Bible!" Numerous individuals have said they were never encouraged to have "a personal relationship with the

Lord" as Catholics. To which I always respond by asking what they see as the reasons for strong promptings to receive Holy Communion frequently, to make visits to Our Lord in the Blessed Sacrament, to pray daily and fervently — if not to foster "a personal relationship with the Lord." The list could go on, but I think you get the point.

If you want to help your friends contemplating a departure from the Church, Bob and Laurie, the most important thing you can do, besides praying for them and with them, is to offer them the joyful example of your own life in the Church. For those who have left, let me suggest the following.

First, tell them we still love them; that we miss them; that we pray for them to come back home.

Second, taking your cue from Pope John Paul II, do not hesitate to apologize for the Church's failures, for poor preaching, for worldly clergy and Religious, for secularizing tendencies, for those theologians and pastors who sound a less-than-certain trumpet. Then go on to encourage them to look beyond our failures and see what Christ sees — the spotless Bride for whom He shed His blood.

Third, remind them that unity is a hallmark of Christ's Church and that those who break that unity bear a serious burden before the Lord (cf. Jn 17; 1 Jn 2:19). It would also be good to share with them the clear teaching of the Second Vatican Council on the necessity of membership in the Church for salvation: "Hence they could not be saved who, knowing that the Catholic Church was founded by God through Christ, would refuse to enter it, or to remain in it."[1]

Fourth, ask them to step outside themselves, to look at what they had as Catholics, and to consider what they now have as Fundamentalists. In all likelihood, any benefit they enjoy could be had within the family of the Church — without the fragmenting of the Body of Christ that occurs with the multiplication of splinter groups. Add to that the wonderful and unique experience of belonging to a Church that truly encompasses "men of every race and tongue, of every people and nation" (Rev 5:9). In what community, other than the Catholic Church, could a gathering of God's People in the hundreds of thousands from every nation on earth proclaim the creed in a common tongue, declaring "that Jesus Christ is Lord, to the glory of God the Father" (Phil 2:11)? Sometimes distance (in this case, from the Church) can create perspective.

Fifth, it might be good to inquire as to why so many Fundamentalists and their preachers seek out Catholics as the objects of their evangelistic efforts. This has been a great mystery to me, especially since approximately one half of the population of the United States is unchurched. Is their interest in Catholics implicit acknowledgment that we do possess the Christian Faith and that their task is thereby made that much easier? Sheep-stealing never makes sense, but it is particularly senseless when millions of others could be given the opportunity to believe if only presented with the Gospel message.

Sixth, ask them — charitably but firmly — how they can claim to have a greater depth of appreciation of the Christian message than two millennia of saints who have gone before us in faith. Perhaps it might even be necessary to recall for them that every sect is ultimately "born in disobedience and pride."[2]

Finally, assure them that even if they are not prepared to "come home" at the present moment, the Church is a loving Mother who is always willing, indeed anxious, to receive back children who have left her bosom. Let them know that their return is a daily intention in your prayers and that you hope you can count on their prayers for us.

Bob and Laurie, God has blessed you with the gift of faith. In keeping with the admonition of the Scriptures, "should anyone ask you the reason for this hope of yours, be ever ready to reply, but speak gently and respectfully" (1 Pt 3:15f). The Lord's gift of faith to you must be acknowledged by your sharing that gift with others. Offer a strong and positive witness. When necessary, "correct those who are confused; the others you must rescue, snatching them from the fire" (Jude 22f).

I make my own the words of the author of the Epistle to the Ephesians (1:15-19):

> From the time I first heard of your faith in the Lord Jesus and your love for the members of the Church, I have never stopped thanking God for you and recommending you in my prayers. May the God of Our Lord Jesus Christ, the Father of glory, grant you a spirit of wisdom and insight to know him clearly. May he enlighten your innermost vision that you may know the great hope to which he has called you, the wealth of his glorious heritage to be distributed among the members of the church, and the immeasurable scope of his power in us who believe.

You and I have different gifts and different vocations within the one Church of Christ, but everything we do must be directed toward the preaching of the Gospel to every creature and the building up of the Church as Christ's Body. In this work of salvation, we need to labor so hard as to suggest that everything depends on us, and to pray so hard as to suggest that everything depends on Almighty God, remembering all the while that our best efforts will be favored with success because it is for the Lord's own Church that we labor and it is He Who has given us the impulse and the grace to be His co-workers. With that realization ever before us, we pray in confidence and joy: "To him whose power now at work in us can do immeasurably more than we ask or imagine — to him be glory in the church and in Christ Jesus through all generations, world without end. Amen" (Eph 3:20f).

God bless and keep you in His love.

In Christ, our Savior,
Father Peter

Appendix: A New Apologetic for Today's Needs

(The following is excerpted from an address dated October 30, 1999, and given by Pope John Paul II to the bishops of Western Canada .)

To teach the Faith and to evangelize is to speak an absolute and universal truth to the world; but it is our duty to speak in appropriate and meaningful ways that make people receptive to that truth. In considering what this entails, [Pope] Paul VI specified four qualities, which he calls *perspicuitas, lenitas, fiducia, prudentia* — clarity, humanity, confidence, and prudence *(Ecclesiam suam,* his encyclical on the Church, no. 81).

To speak with *clarity* means that we must explain comprehensibly the truth of Revelation and the Church's teachings. We should not simply repeat but explain. In other words, we need a new apologetic, geared to the needs of today, which keeps in mind that our task is not just to win arguments but to win souls, to engage not in ideological bickering but to vindicate and promote the Gospel. Such an apologetic will need to find a common "grammar" with those who see things differently and do not share our assumptions, lest we end up speaking different languages even though we may be using the same tongue.

This new apologetic will also need to breathe a spirit of *humanity,* that compassionate humility which understands people's anxieties and questions and which is not quick to presume in them ill will or bad faith. At the same time, it will not yield to a sentimental sense of the love and compassion of Christ sundered from the truth but will insist instead that true love and compassion can make radical demands, precisely because they are inseparable from the truth that alone sets us free (cf. Jn 8:32).

To speak with *confidence* will mean that, however much others may deny us any specific competence or reproach us for the failings of the Church's members, we must never lose sight of the fact that the Gospel of Jesus Christ is the truth for which all people long, no matter how distant, resistant, or hostile they may seem.

And, finally, *prudence,* which [Pope] Paul VI calls practical wisdom and good sense, and which Gregory the Great considers the virtue of the brave, will mean that we give a clear answer to people who ask: "What must we do?" (Lk 3:10, 12, 14). [Pope] Paul VI concluded by affirming that to speak with *perspicuitas, lenitas, fiducia,* and *prudentia* "will make us wise; it will make us teachers" *(Ecclesiam suam,* no. 83). That is what we are called to be above all, dear Brothers, teachers of the truth, who never cease to pray for "the grace to see life whole and the power to speak effectively of it" (Gregory the Great, "On Ezekiel" 1:11:6). What we teach is not a truth of our own devising, but a revealed truth that has come to us through Christ as an incomparable gift. We are sent forth to proclaim this truth and to call those who hear us to what the apostle Paul defines as "the obedience of faith" (Rom 1:5). May the Canadian Martyrs, whose memory you are celebrating with special joy on this 350th anniversary of their death, never cease to teach Christ's faithful in Canada the truth of this obedience and this dying to self in order to live for Christ. May they teach the Church in Canada the mystery of the cross, and may the seed of their sacrifice bear a rich harvest in Canadian hearts! To the intercession of the Virgin Mary, Queen of Apostles and Queen of Martyrs, and to the protection of St. Joseph her spouse, I entrust the entire household of God in your country. Upon you, and upon the priests, women and men Religious, and lay faithful of your Dioceses I cordially bestow my Apostolic Blessing.

Bibliography

Magisterial Sources (Relating to Doctrine, Apologetics, Ecumenism, and Evangelization)

The Catechism of the Catholic Church: Second Edition.

Vatican II, *Lumen Gentium* (Dogmatic Constitution on the Church).

_____, *Unitatis Redintegratio* (Decree on Ecumenism).

_____, *Ad Gentes* (Decree on Missionary Activity).

_____, *Dignitatis Humanae* (Decree on Religious Liberty).

Pope Paul VI, *Evangelii Nuntiandi* (On Evangelization).

Pope John Paul II, *Redemptoris Missio* (On Evangelization).

_____, *Tertio Millennio Adveniente* (On the Coming Third Millennium).

Useful Books

(*Denotes a work by a Catholic author. Some of the volumes listed below by non-Catholics are very fair and helpful in coming to an understanding of the Protestant perspective; others [e.g., Boettner, Hislop] are vitriolic but classics of the genre and, therefore, important to know.)

*Alpha, Veralyn R., *A Heavenly Journey* (Milford, Ohio: Faith Publishing Co., 1994).

Anderson, H. George, et al., eds., *Justification by Faith* (Minneapolis, Minn.: Augsburg Publishing House, 1985).

*Aquilina, Mike, *The Fathers of the Church: An Introduction to the First Christian Teachers* (Huntington, Ind.: Our Sunday Visitor, 1999).

Bainton, Roland H., *The Age of the Reformation* (Princeton, N.J.: D. Van Nostrand Co., Inc., 1956).

*Bertolucci, Rev. John Patrick, *Pastoral Answers to Questions About the Faith* (Huntington, Ind.: Our Sunday Visitor, 1995).

Boettner, Loraine, *Roman Catholicism* (Philadelphia, Pa.: The Presbyterian and Reformed Publishing Co., 1974).

Braaten, Carl E. and Jenson, Robert W., eds., *The Catholicity of the Reformation* (Grand Rapids, Mich.: William B. Eerdmans Publishing Co., 1996).

Brewer, Bartholomew F., *Pilgrimage From Rome* (Greenville, S.C.: Bob Jones University Press, Inc., 1982).

*The Catholic Distance University, *Catholic Apologetics, Course Manual* (Hamilton, Va.: The Catholic Distance University, 1996).

*Catholics Committed to Support the Pope, ed., *Précis of Official Catholic Teaching on Faith, Revelation and the Bible* (Silver Spring, Md.: CCSP, 1990).

*Catoir, John T., *World Religions: Beliefs behind Today's Headlines* (New York: Alba House, 1992).

Coffey, Tony, *Once a Catholic: What You Need to Know about Roman Catholicism* (Eugene, Ore.: Harvest House Publishers, 1993).

Cohen, Norman J., ed. et al., *The Fundamentalist Phenomenon* (Grand Rapids, Mich.: William B. Eerdmans Publishing Co., 1990).

Colson, Charles and Neuhaus, Richard John, *Evangelicals and Catholics: Toward a Common Mission Together* (An Ecumenical Venture) (Dallas, Tex.: Word Publishing, 1995).

The Companion to the Catechism of the Catholic Church (San Francisco: Ignatius Press, 1994).

Cumbey, Constance E., *The Hidden Dangers of the Rainbow: The New Age Movement and Our Coming Age of Barbarism* (Shreveport, La.: Huntington House, Inc., 1983).

*Currie, David B., *Born Fundamentalist, Born Again Catholic* (San Francisco: Ignatius Press, 1996).

*D'Angelo, Louise, *The Catholic Answer to the Jehovah's Witnesses, A Challenge Accepted* (Meriden, Conn.: Maryheart Catholic Information Center, Inc., 1981).

*Duquin, Lorene Hanley, *Could You Ever Come Back to the Catholic Church?* (New York: Alba House, 1997).

The Eerdmans' Handbook to the World's Religions (Grand Rapids, Mich.: William B. Eerdmans Publishing Co., 1994).

*England, Randy, *The Unicorn in the Catholic Church* (Manassas, Va.: Trinity Communications, 1990).

*Epie, Chantal, *Upon This Rock* (New York: Scepter Publishers, Inc., 1991).

*Fox, Rev. Robert J., *Protestant Fundamentalism and the Born Again Catholic* (Alexandria, S.D.: Fatima Family Apostolate, 1991).

*Gambero, Rev. Luigi, *Mary and the Fathers of the Church* (San Francisco: Ignatius Press, 1999).

*Gesy, Rev. Lawrence J., *Today's Destructive Cults and Movements* (Huntington, Ind.: Our Sunday Visitor, 1993).

Gnuse, Robert, *The Authority of the Bible* (New York: Paulist Press, 1985).

*Graham, Henry G., *Where We Got the Bible* (San Diego, Calif.: Catholic Answers, 1997).

*Guindon, Kenneth R., *The King's Highway — El Camino Real: God's Highway to Peace and Happiness* (San Francisco: Ignatius Press, 1996).

*Hampsch, Rev. John H., *Glad You Asked, Scriptural Answers for Our Times* (Huntington, Ind.: Our Sunday Visitor, 1992).

Hislop, Rev. Alexander, *The Two Babylons or the Papal Worship* (Neptune, N.J.: Loizeaux Brothers, 1959).

Hoekema, Anthony A., *The Four Major Cults* (Grand Rapids, Mich.: William B. Eerdmans Publishing Co., 1963).

Hoezee, Scott, *Speaking as One: A Look at the Ecumenical Creeds* (Grand Rapids, Mich.: CRC Publications and William B. Eerdmans Publishing Co., 1997).

*Howard, Thomas, *Evangelical Is Not Enough: Worship of God in Liturgy and Sacrament* (San Francisco: Ignatius Press, 1984).

_____, *On Being Catholic* (San Francisco: Ignatius Press, 1997).

Jurgens, William A., *The Faith of the Early Fathers* (Collegeville, Minn.: Liturgical Press, 1979).

Kaplan, Lawrence, ed., *Fundamentalism in Comparative Perspective* (Amherst: University of Massachusetts Press, 1992).

*Keating, Karl, *Catholicism and Fundamentalism, The Attack on "Romanism" by "Bible Christians"* (San Francisco: Ignatius Press, 1988).

_____, *The Usual Suspects* (San Francisco: Ignatius Press, 2000).

_____, *What Catholics Really Believe* (San Francisco: Ignatius Press, 1992).

Kistler, Don, ed., *Sola Scriptura! The Protestant Position on the Bible* (Morgan, Pa.: Soli Deo Gloria Publications, 1995).

*Klein, Rev. Peter, *Catholic Source Book* (Dubuque, Iowa: Brown Roa Publishing Media [a division of Harcourt Brace & Co.], 1990).

*Kreeft, Peter, *Fundamentals of the Faith: Essays in Christian Apologetics* (San Francisco: Ignatius Press, 1988).

_____, *Yes or No, Straight Answers to Tough Questions about Christianity* (San Francisco: Ignatius Press, 1984).

*LeBar, Rev. James J., *Cults, Sects, and the New Age* (Huntington, Ind.: Our Sunday Visitor, 1989).

Leith, John H., ed., *Creeds of the Churches*, 3rd ed. (Louisville, Ky.: John Knox Press, 1982).

Lewis, C. S., *The Case for Christianity* (New York: The Macmillan Co., 1950).

Lightner, Robert P., *Handbook of Evangelical Theology* (Grand Rapids, Mich.: Kregel Publications, 1995).

*Lord, Bob and Penny, *Cults: Battle of the Angels* (Fair Oaks, Calif.: Journeys of Faith, 1997).

_____, *Tragedy of the Reformation* (Fair Oaks, Calif.: Journeys of Faith, 1997).

Lull, Timothy F., ed., *Martin Luther's Basic Theological Writings* (Minneapolis, Minn.: Fortress Press, 1989).

Lutzer, Erwin, *The Doctrines That Divide* (Grand Rapids, Mich.: Kregel Publications, 1998).

*Madrid, Patrick, *Where Is That in the Bible?* (Huntington, Ind.: Our Sunday Visitor, 2001).

_____, *Any Friend of God's Is a Friend of Mine* (San Diego, Calif.: Basilica Press, 1996).

_____, *Surprised by Truth* (San Diego, Calif.: Basilica Press, 1994).

Mahan, Walter L., *The Unveiling of End-Time Events* (Nashville, Tenn.: Winston-Derek Publishers, Inc., 1993).

*Marks, Frederick W., *A Brief for Belief, The Case for Catholicism* (Santa Barbara, Calif.: Queenship Publishing Co., 1999).

Marsden, George M., *Reforming Fundamentalism* (Grand Rapids, Mich.: William B. Eerdmans Publishing Co., 1987).

_____, *Understanding Fundamentalism and Evangelicalism* (Grand Rapids, Mich.: William B. Eerdmans Publishing Co., 1991).

*Marshall, H. J., *The Church or the Bible?* (Boothwyn, Pa.: Marshall Publishing Co., 1993).

Martin, Dr. Walter, *Essential Christianity, A Handbook of Basic Christian Doctrines* (Ventura, Calif.: Regal Books [a division of Gospel Light Publications], 1980).

*Martin, Ralph, *Is Jesus Coming Soon? A Catholic Perspective on the Second Coming* (San Francisco: Ignatius Press, 1997).

*Mbukanma, Rev. Jude O., *Is It in the Bible?* (Clifton, Va.: MET Publishing, 1994).

*Miller, Rev. J. Michael, *Life's Greatest Grace: Why I Belong to the Catholic Church* (Huntington, Ind.: Our Sunday Visitor, 1993).

*Mirus, Jeffrey, ed., *Reasons for Hope, Apologetics* (Front Royal, Va.: Christendom Publications, 1982).

*Myers, Rawley, *Faith Experiences of Catholic Converts* (Huntington, Ind.: Our Sunday Visitor, 1992).

*National Conference of Catholic Bishops, *A Pastoral Statement on Biblical Fundamentalism* (Washington, D.C.: United States Catholic Conference, 1987).

*Neuner, J. and Dupuis, J., eds., *The Christian Faith* (New York: Alba House, 1996).

*Noll, Archbishop John Francis, *Father Smith Instructs Jackson*, rev. ed. (Huntington, Ind.: Our Sunday Visitor, 1975).

*O'Brien, Rev. John A., *The Faith of Millions* (Huntington, Ind.: Our Sunday Visitor, 1974).

*Ott, Ludwig, *Fundamentals of Catholic Dogma* (Rockford, Ill.: TAN Books, 1974).

*Pennock, Michael, *Your Faith and You, A Synthesis of Catholic Belief* (Notre Dame, Ind.: Ave Maria Press, 1986).

*Pontifical Biblical Commission, *The Interpretation of the Bible in the Church* (Boston, Mass.: St. Paul Books and Media, 1993).

*Ramsey, Rev. Boniface, *Beginning to Read the Fathers* (New York: Paulist Press, 1985).

*Ray, Stephen K., *Crossing the Tiber: Evangelical Protestants Discover the Historic Church* (San Francisco: Ignatius Press, 1997).

_____, *Upon This Rock* (San Francisco: Ignatius Press, 1999).

*Ryan, Rev. Kenneth, *Catholic Questions, Catholic Answers* (Ann Arbor, Mich.: Servant Publications, 1989).

*Sadowski, Rev. Frank, ed., *The Church Fathers on the Bible* (New York: Alba House, 1987).

*Saliba, Rev. John A., *Understanding New Religious Movements* (Grand Rapids, Mich.: William B. Eerdmans Publishing Co., 1995).

*Schreck, Alan, *An Explanation of Commonly Misunderstood Catholic Beliefs* (Ann Arbor, Mich.: Servant Books, 1984).

Schrotenboer, Paul G., ed., *Roman Catholicism: A Contemporary Evangelical Perspective* (Grand Rapids, Mich.: Baker Book House, 1992).

*Shea, Mark P., *By What Authority? An Evangelical Discovers Catholic Tradition* (Huntington, Ind.: Our Sunday Visitor, 1996).

_____, *This Is My Body: An Evangelical Discovers the Real Presence* (Front Royal, Va.: Christendom Press, 1993).

*Sheed, Frank and Ward, Maisie, *Catholic Evidence Training Outlines* (Ann Arbor, Mich.: Catholic Evidence Guild, 1992 [1940]).

Sproul, R. C., *Essential Truths of the Christian Faith* (Wheaton, Ill.: Tyndale House Publishers, Inc., 1992).

*Stravinskas, Very Rev. Peter M. J., *The Bible and the Mass: Understanding the Scriptural Basis of the Liturgy*, rev. ed. (Mount Pocono, Pa.: Newman House Press, 2000).

_____, *The Catholic Answer Book of Mary* (Huntington, Ind.: Our Sunday Visitor, 2000).

_____, *The Catholic Answer Books I, II, III* (Huntington, Ind.: Our Sunday Visitor, 1990/1994/1998).

_____, *The Catholic Church and the Bible* (San Francisco: Ignatius Press, 1996).

_____, *The Catholic Dictionary* (Huntington, Ind.: Our Sunday Visitor, 1993).

_____, *The Catholic Encyclopedia* (Huntington, Ind.: Our Sunday Visitor, 1998).

_____, *A Catholic Understanding of the Gospels* (Huntington, Ind.: Our Sunday Visitor, 1992).

_____, *Mary and the Fundamentalist Challenge* (Huntington, Ind.: Our Sunday Visitor, 1998).

_____, *The Mass: A Biblical Prayer* (Huntington, Ind.: Our Sunday Visitor, 1989).

_____, *La Sicología y Métodos de Proselitismo* (Huntington, Ind.: Our Sunday Visitor, 1997).

_____, *A Tour of the Catholic Catechism* (Libertyville, Ill.: Marytown Press, 1996).

_____, *Understanding the Sacraments: A Guide for Prayer and Study* (San Francisco: Ignatius Press, 1997).

_____, *What Catholics Believe about Mary* (Huntington, Ind.: Our Sunday Visitor, 1988).

Strozier, Charles B., *Apocalypse, On the Psychology of Fundamentalism in America* (Boston, Mass.: Beacon Press, 1994).

*Sungenis, Robert A., *Not by Faith Alone* (Santa Barbara, Calif.: Queenship Publishing Co., 1996).

_____, *Not by Scripture Alone* (Santa Barbara, Calif.: Queenship Publishing Co., 1997).

Swaggart, Jimmy, *Catholicism and Christianity* (Baton Rouge, La.: Jimmy Swaggart Ministries, 1986).

*Vilar, Rev. Juan Diaz, S.J., *Religious Sects: A Summary of Their Basic Beliefs* (New York: Catholic Book Publishing Co., 1992).

*Whalen, William J., *Strange Gods: Contemporary Religious Cults in America* (Huntington, Ind.: Our Sunday Visitor, 1981).

White, James R., *Answers to Catholic Claims: A Discussion of Biblical Authority* (Southbridge, Mass.: Crown Publications, Inc., 1990).

*Working Group on New Religious Movements, The, *Sects and New Religious Movements* (Washington, D.C.: United States Catholic Conference, 1995).

*Zolli, Eugenio, *Why I Became a Catholic* (Fort Collins, Colo.: Roman Catholic Books, 1953).

Worthwhile Periodicals

- The Catholic Answer *(1-800-348-2440, Our Sunday Visitor)*
- Envoy *(1-800-55ENVOY)*
- Lay Witness *(1-800-693-2484)*
- This Rock *(1-619-387-7200)*

Internet Resources

- *www.cin.org (Catholic Information Network)*
- *www.osv.com (*The Catholic Answer, *Our Sunday Visitor)*
- *www.newadvent.org (An apologetics Web page)*
- *www.vatican.va (The official Holy See Web page)*
- *www.vatican.va/news_services/press/vis/vis_en.html (Vatican Information Service)*

Notes

Introduction

1. The Fathers of the Church are those theologians from the earliest centuries of Christianity who grappled with the major doctrines of the Catholic Faith and offered answers of substance and value. Among them, one would list Jerome, Irenaeus, Augustine, Hippolytus, Leo the Great, Hilary, and Epiphanius.

2. The Magisterium is the teaching authority of the Church. Statements of popes and ecumenical councils are included in this source of authoritative teaching.

3. *Apologia pro Vita Sua* (1864), "Position of my Mind since 1845."

4. Throughout this work the reader will note frequent mention of the Reverend Jimmy Swaggart. This should not be interpreted as an attack on the man himself, a questioning of his sincerity, or a failure to respect his freedom of conscience to believe and act as he feels the Lord directs him. Mr. Swaggart has served as the point of reference, however, because in his writings and in his preaching, he typifies the classic tone and content of Fundamentalist evangelists. While most of the Fundamentalist objections to the Catholic Faith are voiced from pulpits, Mr. Swaggart committed his to writing, thereby making an organized, coherent response more possible.

Chapter 1

1. For an excellent statement of this, see Vatican II's Dogmatic Constitution on Divine Revelation (*Dei Verbum*), nn. 9 and 10.

2. Jimmy Swaggart, "A Letter to My Catholic Friends," *The Evangelist*, January 1983, pp. 4-17.

3. John Henry Cardinal Newman in his *Essay on the Development of Church Doctrine* spoke of change in this way: "In a higher world, it is otherwise, but here below, to live is to change, and to be perfect is to have changed often."

4. *Contra epistolam Manichaei,* 5, 6: PL 42, 176.

5. Dogmatic Constitution on Divine Revelation (*Dei Verbum*), n. 21.

Chapter 2

1. Some versions translate the Greek word *"anothen"* as "again"; the *New American Bible* renders *"anothen"* as "from above." The word can mean either; the misunderstanding comes out in the text as Nicodemus (in v. 4) takes it to mean "again," and Jesus uses the confusion to explain the nature of salvation. Catholic theology has no problem, however, with taking both occurrences of the word to be "again"; for the sake of discussion, that is precisely what I do here.

2. Jimmy Swaggart, "A Letter to My Catholic Friends," *The Evangelist,* January 1983, p. 16.

3. Ibid., p. 8.

Chapter 3

1. Dogmatic Constitution on the Church (*Lumen Gentium*), n. 8: "This Church, constituted and organized as a society in the present world, subsists in the Catholic Church, which is governed by the successor of Peter and the bishops in communion with him." Further, "they could not be saved who, knowing that the Catholic Church was founded as necessary by God through Christ, would refuse either to enter it, or to remain in it" (n. 14).

2. Exceptionally noteworthy in this regard is *The Decline and Fall of the Roman Empire* by the anti-Catholic historian Edward Gibbon, but it is also apparent in a standard college text like Crave Brinton's *History of Civilization.* Even non-Catholic ecclesiastical historians recognize this; see, for example, Henry Chadwick in *The Early Church* or J. G. Davies in *The Early Christian Church.*

3. Decree on Ecumenism (*Unitatis Redintegratio*), n. 11.

Chapter 4

1. Dogmatic Constitution on the Church (*Lumen Gentium*), n. 20.

2. Cf. 2 Timothy 1:6, 2 Timothy 2:2, 1 Timothy 5:22; Titus 1:5ff.

3. Some Fundamentalists argue that the Catholic claim that Jesus established His Church on Peter is erroneous, and that the correct interpretation is that Jesus established His Church on the confession of Peter's faith and not on Peter himself. The two go hand in hand, for it was Peter the man of faith who had been specially chosen to enunciate the doctrine of faith that had been given to him by a special divine revelation, according to Matthew 16:17. Therefore, the Father specifically chose Peter to give voice to the doctrine of His Son's Messiahship.

4. Cf. Raymond E. Brown, et al. (eds.), *Peter in the New Testament* (New York: Paulist Press, 1973).

5. *Pastor Aeternus,* Chapter 4.

6. Dogmatic Constitution on the Church (*Lumen Gentium*), n. 25.

7. *Adversus Haereses.*

8. It is well known that there was a doctrinal Inquisition and a political Inquisition. Frequently the State used the findings of the doctrinal Inquisition to justify punishment of citizens who were not just religiously unorthodox but also politically divisive or dangerous. Indeed, the threat to political unity posed by doctrinal dissidents was a prime influence in the promotion of the Inquisition by civil authorities.

Chapter 5

1. Jimmy Swaggart, "A Letter to My Catholic Friends," *The Evangelist,* January 1983, p. 12.

2. The *Revised Standard Version* translation makes this point even more clearly when it says that Timothy received his gift "*through* the laying on of my hands . . ." (emphasis added).

3. The Sacrament of Holy Orders also includes deacons and bishops, whose ministries are not discussed here because the diaconate is generally accepted by Fundamentalists and because the office of bishop flows from that of priest; if the priesthood is not accepted, the episcopacy makes no sense, since it is viewed as the "fullness of the priesthood."

It should be noted that the Greek word used for the elders of the Christian community is *"presbyteroi"* (presbyters), whence comes our English word "priests."

4. Of course, if the Eucharist is not regarded as a sacrifice but only a memorial meal, no priesthood is needed. For a discussion of the sacrificial aspect of the Eucharist, see Chapter 7.

5. Some critics charge that priestly celibacy was an innovation of the medieval Church. This is not the case. The Council of Elvira (c. 300) already spoke of celibacy as a "tradition."

It should also be noted that even though marriage was not always forbidden to clergy, there were strong prohibitions against sexual intercourse for clergy (even with their wives) from the earliest times.

6. Swaggart, ibid.

7. The Church does not "forbid marriage." Rather, she calls to the priesthood only those men who give evidence of the charism of celibacy and who are prepared to renounce freely the right to marry for the sake of the kingdom.

8. Interestingly enough, the *Revised Standard Version* translation is even more explicit as it says: "I became your father in Christ Jesus through the gospel."

9. Dogmatic Constitution on the Church (*Lumen Gentium*), n. 10.

Chapter 6

1. Cf. J. Neville Ward, *Five for Sorrow, Ten for Joy* (Garden City, N.Y.: Doubleday, 1974).

2. For a good ecumenical discussion, see: Raymond E. Brown, et al. (eds.), *Mary in the New Testament* (New York: Paulist Press, 1978).

3. The literary figure of speech known as "inclusion" is a device whereby an incident begins and ends in the same way. Luke, for example, begins and ends his Gospel with divine intervention as a way of demonstrating the presence of the divine throughout.

4. For examples of intercessory prayer in the New Testament, see Colossians 1:9, 2 Thessalonians 1:11, 2 Thessalonians 3:1, and James 5:16.

5. The mysteries are divided into joyful (Annunciation, Visitation, Nativity, Presentation in the Temple, Finding in the Temple); sorrowful (Agony in the Garden, Scourging at the Pillar, Crowning with Thorns, Carrying of the Cross, Crucifixion); and glorious (Resurrection, Ascension, Descent of the Holy Spirit, Mary's Assumption, Mary's Glorification in Heaven).

6. It should be noted that one of the oldest shrines in the Holy Land is the Church of the Dormition, the spot venerated as the place from which Mary was assumed into heaven. This church dates back to the sixth century A.D., and there is evidence that the liturgical feast was celebrated as early as the fifth century. This insight is important to grasp, since some people question the validity of the doctrine because it was defined as a dogma of faith by Pope Pius XII in 1950. Again, one needs to recall that dogmatic definition only means that something was always believed but is now being solemnly proclaimed as a part of the Faith.

7. Jimmy Swaggart, "A Letter to My Catholic Friends," *The Evangelist*, January 1983, p. 13.

8. For example, 2 Samuel 6:23 says that "Michal the daughter of Saul had no child to the day of her death." One can no more argue that the use of "to/until" by Matthew implies Mary's having a child after the birth of Jesus than one can say that "to/until" indicates that Michal had a child after her dying day.

9. Zwingli saw Ezekiel 44 as proof of Mary's perpetual virginity.

10. If Jesus had other siblings, why would He entrust His Mother to the Beloved Disciple as He was dying on the cross?

11. For example, Paul encountered Christ on the road to Damascus (cf. Acts 9:3ff), and Peter had a vision of an angel leading him from prison (cf. Acts 12:7).

12. Interestingly enough, the Church does not require Catholics to accept such apparitions as necessary for belief. The same is true of the use of medals, scapulars, novenas, etc. All of these things are available to Catholics if they help foster a life of faith but are not mandatory practices.

13. "Canonization" is the process by which, after extensive

investigation of a believer's life and witness, he or she is declared to have lived a life worthy of being called a saint and of having his or her name added to the "canon" of saints.

Chapter 7

1. Samuel Terrien, *The Elusive Presence* (New York: Harper and Row Publications, 1983).

2. Swaggart, "A Letter to My Catholic Friends," *The Evangelist*, January 1983, p. 12.

3. Frank Burr Marsh and Hargy J. Leon (eds.), *Tacitus: Selections from His Works* (Norman: University of Oklahoma Press, 1963), p. 146.

4. Donald Dudley, *The World of Tacitus* (London: Secker and Warburg, 1968), p. 166.

5. Swaggart, ibid.

6. Ibid.

Chapter 8

1. Swaggart, "A Letter to My Catholic Friends," *The Evangelist*, January 1983, p. 10.

2. Ibid., p. 11.

3. The complete text of the formula of absolution prayed over the penitent by the priest reads as follows: "God, the Father of mercies, / through the death and resurrection of his Son / has reconciled the world to himself / and sent the Holy Spirit among us / for the forgiveness of sins; / through the ministry of the Church / may God give you pardon and peace, / and I absolve you from your sins / in the name of the Father, and of the Son, / and of the Holy Spirit."

4. Swaggart, p. 16.

5. Ibid., p. 14.

Chapter 9

1. Swaggart, "A Letter to My Catholic Friends," *The Evangelist*, January 1983, p. 15.

2. Ibid., p. 14.

3. Does the rich man's crying out "Father Abraham" suggest

the invocation of a saint as well as calling another human being "father"? If so, we find examples in Scripture of two practices that Fundamentalists view as troublesome.

4. Of course, we speak in analogous, anthropomorphic terms here.

5. One must admit that at times in the history of the Church, genuine abuses surfaced in this practice, especially in pre-Reformation Germany. These abuses were condemned and corrected at the Council of Trent.

6. Swaggart, p. 14.

7. The last two inscriptions likewise support another point of contention between Catholics and Fundamentalists, namely, the antiquity and validity of invoking or seeking the intercession of the saints.

8. Cf. R. J. Zwi Werblowsky and Geoffrey Wigoder, "Mourning," in *The Encyclopedia of the Jewish Religion* (New York: Holt, Rinehart and Winston, Inc., 1965), p. 273f.

Epilogue
1. Dogmatic Constitution on the Church (*Lumen Gentium*), n. 14.

2. Thomas J. Barbarie, "An Open Letter to Jimmy Swaggart," in *The Catholic Commentator,* January 12, 1983.

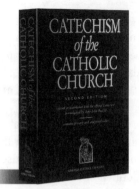